TOUCHSTONE

TOUCH THE EARTH
A Self-Portrait of Indian Existence

by
T. C. McLUHAN

photographs by
EDWARD S. CURTIS

A TOUCHSTONE BOOK
PUBLISHED BY SIMON & SCHUSTER, INC.

A Touchstone Book
Published by Simon & Schuster, Inc.
Simon & Schuster Building
Rockefeller Center
1230 Avenue of the Americas
New York, New York 10020
TOUCHSTONE and colophon are registered trademarks
of Simon & Schuster, Inc.

Reprinted by arrangement with Outerbridge & Lazard
ISBN 0-671-22275-9

Manufactured in the United States of America

9   10   11   12   13   14   15

CONTENTS

ACKNOWLEDGMENTS

I would like to gratefully acknowledge the help, advice and encouragement I received in compiling this book from the following people:

Arley Bondarin for his assistance in collecting the photographs; Dr. Edmund Carpenter who pointed out unusual and interesting passages, Jim Davey of Ottawa and Sol Lewis of New York; the librarians and their assistants at the New York Public Library for their tremendous co-operation and help; Jim MacNeil of the Dept. of Indian Affairs, Ottawa; Dr. Ed Rogers of the Royal Ontario Museum, Toronto; and Dr. Sam Stanley of the Smithsonian Institute, Washington.

My special thanks to Geoffrey for all his encouragement and patience without which I would never have completed the book.

INTRODUCTION:
THE SPIRIT OF THE EARTH

The pain of the Indian, as he experienced the death of his way of life, has not been fully understood by the white man, and perhaps never will. When Black Elk, a holy man of the Oglala Sioux, speaks of "the beauty and strangeness of the earth" he speaks of reverence for the everyday environment, an environment that was integrally interwoven with Indian life. When the wild herds were killed, and the sacred lands of their ancestors over-run, then at least one form of the will and spirit of the Indian nations dwindled and died. Who the Indians were, could not without serious loss be separated from where and how they lived.

In this book, the Indians speak for themselves, of the quality of their life. The passages which make up the book have been taken from the speeches and, more recently, the writings of Indians living in all parts of the North American continent, between the sixteenth and the twentieth centuries. They speak with courtesy and respect of the land, of animals, of the objects which made up the territory in which they lived. They saw no virtue in imposing their will over their environment: private acquisition, almost without exception, was to them a way to poverty, not to riches. The meaning of their life was identified through their relationships with each other and their homelands — all of which was given depth and resonance by memory.

A Wintu woman, living in California about fifteen years ago, close to an area where white men were mining gold by means of hydraulic processes and blasting, commented: "When we burn grass for grasshoppers, we don't ruin things. We shake down acorns and pinenuts. But the White people plow up the ground, pull down the trees, kill everything.... They blast rocks and scatter them on the ground.... How can the spirit of the earth like the White man?... Everywhere the White man has touched it, it is sore." The same attitude is reflected in a recent letter from the religious leaders of the Hopi Nation to the President of the United States, reprinted here in section four.

Many of the passages in this book represented the Indians' attempts to offer their ideas to the white man, either as a gift or in the hope that through understanding the white man would let the Indian be. As Indians saw more of the white man's ways, their tone of voice became mystified, angry, desperate and, finally, empty of hope.

It is easy now for all of us, not Indians, to feel a vicarious rage and misery on their behalf. The Indians, dead or alive, would justly receive such feelings with pity and contempt. It is too easy to feel sympathy for a people whose culture has been wrecked. This book has been compiled with respect and, I hope, with courtesy, so that once again the Indians may speak in their own voice.

It is well understood that the only decent future for us who live in America now is through a rediscovery of our environment. We need to establish a right relationship with the land and its resources; otherwise, the destruction of the Indian will be followed by the destruction of nature; and in the destruction of nature will follow the destruction of ourselves.

The Indians, in a sense, knew this all along. For many generations they learned how to live in America, in a state of balance; or, as a Christian would say, in a state of grace. Perhaps now, after hundreds of years of ignoring their wisdom, we may learn from the Indians.

This is not a scholarly book. Some passages in it are well-known, but too vital to leave out. Most have been found in books, manuscripts and papers of varying obscurity. The provenance of some is a matter of doubt or dispute among scholars; in these cases, sometimes indicated in the text, the version most in accord with available information has been used.

The pictures in this book were taken by Edward S. Curtis in the early years of this century under the patronage and support of J. Pierpont Morgan and President Roosevelt. Curtis spent many years recording with extraordinary photographic skill a people and a way of life he knew were doomed to extinction.

I THE MORNING SUN, THE NEW SWEET EARTH AND THE GREAT SILENCE

We always had plenty; our children never cried from hunger, neither were our people in want. . . . The rapids of Rock River furnished us with an abundance of excellent fish, and the land being very fertile, never failed to produce good crops of corn, beans, pumpkins, and squashes. . . . Here our village stood for more than a hundred years, during all of which time we were the undisputed possessors of the Mississippi Valley. . . . Our village was healthy and there was no place in the country possessing such advantages, nor hunting grounds better than those we had in possession. If a prophet had come to our village in those days and told us that the things were to take place which have since come to pass, none of our people would have believed him.

Ma-ka-tai-me-she-kia-kiak,
or Black Hawk, Chief of the
Sauk and Fox

Cañon de Chelly, Navajo

Holy Mother Earth, the trees and all nature, are
witnesses of your thoughts and deeds.

A Winnebago wise saying

We love quiet; we suffer the mouse to play; when the
woods are rustled by the wind, we fear not.

Indian Chief to the governor
of Pennsylvania, 1796

Born in 1868, Chief Luther Standing Bear spent his early years on the plains of Nebraska and South Dakota. At the age of 11, he was one of the first students to enroll at the Indian school at Carlisle, Pennsylvania, which was established in 1879. After four years at the school, he became a teacher and taught at the Rosebud Reservation in South Dakota. He joined Buffalo Bill's Wild West Show as an interpreter in 1898 and spent his later years lecturing and writing. In his statement, Chief Standing Bear speaks of the Lakota, which is the tribal name of the western bands of Plains people now known as the Sioux (the eastern bands call themselves the Dakotas). Lakota tends to be used interchangeably with Dakota.

THE LAKOTA WAS A TRUE NATURIST — A LOVER OF NATURE. He loved the earth and all things of the earth, the attachment growing with age. The old people came literally to love the soil and they sat or reclined on the ground with a feeling of being close to a mothering power. It was good for the skin to touch the earth and the old people liked to remove their moccasins and walk with bare feet on the sacred earth. Their tipis were built upon the earth and their altars were made of earth. The birds that flew in the air came to rest upon the earth and it was the final abiding place of all things that lived and grew. The soil was soothing, strengthening, cleansing and healing.

That is why the old Indian still sits upon the earth instead of propping himself up and away from its life-giving forces. For him, to sit or lie upon the ground is to be able to think more deeply and to feel more keenly; he can see more clearly into the mysteries of life and come closer in kinship to other lives about him. . . .

Kinship with all creatures of the earth, sky and water was a real and active principle. For the animal and bird world there existed a brotherly feeling that kept the Lakota safe among them and so close did some of the Lakotas come to their feathered and furred friends that in true brotherhood they spoke a common tongue.

The old Lakota was wise. He knew that man's heart away from nature becomes hard; he knew that lack of respect for growing, living things soon led to lack of respect for humans too. So he kept his youth close to its softening influence.

6

Ohiyesa, or Charles Eastman, a Santee Dakota physician and author, was born in 1858 near Redwood Falls, Minnesota. Four years later, after the Minnesota Massacre in 1862, he fled with his uncle to Canada where he lived the nomadic life of the Sioux until he was 15. In 1887 he graduated from Dartmouth College and three years later received a degree in medicine from Boston University. He served 3 years as a government physician to the Pine Ridge Agency, South Dakota, during the ghost dance disturbances, and afterwards turned to private practice. About this time he began to write and lecture; his first book, *Indian Boyhood,* appeared in 1902. Ohiyesa is perhaps the most famous of American Indian authors. He died in 1939.

I KNOW THAT OUR PEOPLE POSSESSED REMARKABLE POWERS OF concentration and abstraction, and I sometimes fancy that such nearness to nature as I have described keeps the spirit sensitive to impressions not commonly felt, and in touch with the unseen powers. Some of us seemed to have a peculiar intuition for the locality of a grave, which they explained by saying that they had received a communication from the spirit departed. My own grandmother was one of these, and as far back as I can remember, when camping in a strange country, my brother and I would search for and find human bones at the spot she had indicated to us as an ancient burial place or the spot where a lone warrior had fallen. Of course, the outward signs of burial had been long since obliterated.

The occasion for this speech was an Indian council in the Valley of Walla Walla in 1855, presided over by Isaac Stevens, governor of Washington Territory, and General Palmer, superintendent of Indian Affairs for Oregon. Governor Steven's objectives were to set up three reservations: one for the Cayuses, the Walla-Wallas and Umatillas; a second for the Nez Perces; and a third for the Yakimas. Young Chief, of the Cayuses, opposed the treaty and grounded his objections on the fact that the Indians had no right to sell the ground which the Great Spirit had given for their support. He gave the following speech before signing away their land.

I WONDER IF THE GROUND HAS ANYTHING TO SAY? I WONDER if the ground is listening to what is said? I wonder if the ground would come alive and what is on it? Though I hear what the ground says. The ground says, It is the Great Spirit that placed me here. The Great Spirit tells me to take care of the Indians, to feed them aright. The Great Spirit appointed the roots to feed the Indians on. The water says the same thing. The Great Spirit directs me, Feed the Indians well. The grass says the same thing, Feed the Indians well. The ground, water and grass say, The Great Spirit has given us our names. We have these names and hold these names. The ground says, The Great Spirit has placed me here to produce all that grows on me, trees and fruit. The same way the ground says, It was from me man was made. The Great Spirit, in placing men on the earth, desired them to take good care of the ground and to do each other no harm. . . .

Travaux-Piegan

In 1859 the United States Senate ratified the treaty signed with the Yakima Indians at Walla Walla in 1855. The treaty gave to the Indians the possession of certain land, but ceded other portions of it to the United States. The Supreme Court, on a test case, repudiated the treaty (by a divided vote) in favor of the Indians. Another test case was taken up. In testimony therein Chief Weninock of the Yakimas made the statement (in about 1915) quoted here. Ultimately, the Indians gained their point, which was to be allowed to fish unmolested at their accustomed fishing places.

GOD CREATED THE INDIAN COUNTRY AND IT WAS LIKE HE spread out a big blanket. He put the Indians on it. They were created here in this Country, truly honest, and that was the time this river started to run. Then God created fish in this river and put deer in the mountains and made laws through which has come the increase of fish and game. Then the Creator gave us Indians Life; we walked, and as soon as we saw the game and fish we knew they were made for us. For the women God made roots and berries to gather, and the Indians grew and multiplied as a people.

When we were created we were given our ground to live on and from this time these were our rights. This is all true. We had the fish before the Missionaries came, before the white man came. We were put here by the Creator and these were our rights as far as my memory to my grandfather. This was the food on which we lived. My mother gathered berries; my father fished and killed the game. These words are mine and they are true. My strength is from the fish; my blood is from the fish, from the roots and berries. The fish and game are the essence of my life. I was not brought from a foreign country and did not come here. I was put here by the Creator.

We had no cattle, no hogs, no grain, only berries and roots and game and fish. We never thought that we would be troubled about these things, and I tell you my people, and I believe it, it is not wrong for us to get this food. Whenever the seasons open I raise my heart in thanks to the Creator of His bounty that this food has come.

I want this treaty to show the officers what our fishing rights were. I was at the Council at Walla Walla with my father, who was one of the Chiefs who signed the treaty. I well remember hearing the talk about the treaty. There were more Indians there at Walla Walla than ever came together at any one place in this country. Besides the women and children, there were two thousand Indian Warriors, and they were there for about one moon, during the same part of the year as now, in May and June.

The Indians and Commissioners were many days talking about making the treaty. One day Governor Stevens read what he had written down and had one of the interpreters explain it to the Indians. After everybody had talked and Pu-Pu-Mox-Mox had talked, General Stevens wanted to hear from the head Chief of the Yakimas. He said "Kamiaken, the great Chief of the Yakimas, has not spoken at all. His people have had no voice here today. He is not afraid to speak — let him speak out."

Something has been said about more and more whites coming into the Indian Country and then the Indians would be driven away from their hunting grounds and fishing places. Then Governor Stevens told the Indians that when the white man came here the rights of the Indians would be protected.

Then Chief Kamiaken said, "I am afraid that the white men are not speaking straight; that their children will not do what is right by our children; that they will not do what you have promised for them."

A great hunter, brave warrior and eloquent spokesman, Crowfoot was born in 1821 at Blackfoot Crossing on the Bow River, now territory in the province of Alberta, Canada. He quickly rose as the orator for the Blackfoot Confederacy. In September 1877, on behalf of his nation, he unwillingly, but trustfully, ceded 50,000 square miles of its prairie land to the Canadian government, a treaty which led to the rapid disappearance of the buffalo, and the near starvation of the Blackfeet. In April of 1890, in his dying hours, his last words were of life.

WHAT IS LIFE? IT IS THE FLASH OF A FIREFLY IN THE NIGHT. IT IS the breath of a buffalo in the winter time. It is the little shadow which runs across the grass and loses itself in the Sunset.

Washing Wheat, San Juan

Porcupine, Cheyenne

The great care with which so many of the Indians utilized every portion of the carcass of a hunted animal," writes anthropologist Dorothy Lee, "was an expression, not of economic thrift, but of courtesy and respect; in fact, an aspect of the religious relationship to the slain." The Wintu Indians of California lived on very densely wooded land where it was difficult even to find clear land to erect houses. "Nevertheless," continues Lee, "they would use only dead wood for fuel, out of respect for nature." In the following passage, an old holy Wintu woman speaks sadly about the needless destruction of the land in which she lived — a place where gold mining and particularly hydraulic mining had torn up the earth.

THE WHITE PEOPLE NEVER CARED FOR LAND OR DEER OR BEAR. When we Indians kill meat, we eat it all up. When we dig roots we make little holes. When we built houses, we make little holes. When we burn grass for grasshoppers, we don't ruin things. We shake down acorns and pinenuts. We don't chop down the trees. We only use dead wood. But the White people plow up the ground, pull down the trees, kill everything. The tree says, "Don't. I am sore. Don't hurt me." But they chop it down and cut it up. The spirit of the land hates them. They blast out trees and stir it up to its depths. They saw up the trees. That hurts them. The Indians never hurt anything, but the White people destroy all. They blast rocks and scatter them on the ground. The rock says, "Don't. You are hurting me." But the White people pay no attention. When the Indians use rocks, they take little round ones for their cooking. . . . How can the spirit of the earth like the White man? . . . Everywhere the White man has touched it, it is sore.

Tatanka-ohitika, or Brave Buffalo, a Sioux Indian, was a prominent medicine man of the Standing Rock Reservation, as had been his father. Tatanka-ohitika was born near the present site of Pollock, North Dakota, and at the age of 73, in 1911, he described his dream of the sacred stone, large stones having religious value among the Sioux. Tatanka-ohitika speaks of Wakan tanka, the Sioux term for the higher being that is the source of all things. Wakan means mysterious, tanka great. "The exact significance of the term in the mind of the Sioux," Frances Densmore explains (in *Teton Sioux Music),* "is as difficult to formulate as the exact meaning of the word God in the mind of Christians."°

WHEN I WAS TEN YEARS OF AGE I LOOKED AT THE LAND AND the rivers, the sky above, and the animals around me and could not fail to realize that they were made by some great power. I was so anxious to understand this power that I questioned the trees and the bushes. It seemed as though the flowers were staring at me, and I wanted to ask them "Who made you?" I looked at the moss-covered stones; some of them seemed to have the features of a man, but they could not answer me. Then I had a dream, and in my dream one of these small round stones appeared to me and told me that the maker of all was Wakan tanka, and that in order to honor him I must honor his works in nature. The stone said that by my search I had shown myself worthy of supernatural help. It said that if I were curing a sick person I might ask its assistance, and that all the forces of nature would help me work a cure.

°The circular superscript signifies that an additional note or comment appears at the end of the book.

It is significant that certain stones are not found buried in the earth, but are on the top of high buttes. They are round, like the sun and moon, and we know that all things which are round are related to each other. Things which are alike in their nature grow to look like each other, and these stones have lain there a long time, looking at the sun. Many pebbles and stones have been shaped in the current of a stream, but these stones were found far from the water and have been exposed only to the sun and the wind. The earth contains many thousand such stones hidden beneath its surface. The thunderbird is said to be related to these stones, and when a man or an animal is to be punished, the thunderbird strikes the person, and if it were possible to follow the course of the lightning, one of these stones would be found embedded in the earth. Some believe that these stones descend with the lightning, but I believe they are on the ground and are projected downward by the bolt. In all my life I have been faithful to the sacred stones. I have lived according to their requirements, and they have helped me in all my troubles. I have tried to qualify myself as well as possible to handle these sacred stones, yet I know that I am not worthy to speak to Wakan tanka. I make my request of the stones and they are my intercessors.

Okute, or Shooter, an old Teton Sioux, in speaking in 1911 about his holy beliefs, explains that his people believed in a mysterious power whose greatest manifestation was nature, one representation of which was the sun. Adds Redbird, a member of the same tribe, "we made sacrifices to the sun, and our petitions were granted."

ALL LIVING CREATURES AND ALL PLANTS DERIVE THEIR LIFE from the sun. If it were not for the sun, there would be darkness and nothing could grow — the earth would be without life. Yet the sun must have the help of the earth. If the sun alone were to act upon animals and plants, the heat would be so great that they would die, but there are clouds that bring rain, and the action of the sun and earth together supply the moisture that is needed for life. The roots of a plant go down, and the deeper they go the more moisture they find. This is according to the laws of nature and is one of the evidences of the wisdom of Wakan tanka. Plants are sent by Wakan tanka and come from the ground at his command, the part to be affected by the sun and rain appearing above the ground and the roots pressing downward to find the moisture which is supplied for them. Animals and plants are taught by Wakan tanka what they are to do. Wakan tanka teaches the birds to make nests, yet the nests of all birds are not alike. Wakan tanka gives them merely the outline. Some make better nests than others. In the same way some animals are satisfied with very rough dwellings, while others make attractive places in which to live. Some animals also take better care of their young than others. The forest is the home of many birds and other animals, and the water is the home of fish and reptiles. All birds, even those of the same species, are not alike, and it is the same with animals and with human beings. The reason Wakan tanka does not make two birds, or animals, or human beings exactly alike is because each is placed here by Wakan tanka to be an independent individuality and to rely on itself. Some animals are made to live in the ground. The stones and the minerals are placed in the ground by Wakan tanka, some stones being more exposed than others. When a medicine man says that he talks with the sacred stones, it is because of all the substance in the ground these are the ones which most often appear in dreams and are able to communicate with men.

From my boyhood I have observed leaves, trees, and grass, and I have never found two alike. They may have a general likeness, but on examination I have found that they differ slightly. Plants are of different families. . . . It is the same with animals. . . . It is the same with human beings; there is some place which is best adapted to each. The seeds of the plants are blown about by the wind until they reach the place where they will grow best — where the action of the sun and the presence of moisture are most favorable to them, and there they take root and grow. All living creatures and all plants are a benefit to something. Certain animals fulfill their purpose by definite acts. The crows, buzzards and flies are somewhat similar in their use, and even the snakes have purpose in being. In the early days the animals probably roamed over a very wide country until they found a proper place. An animal depends a great deal on the natural conditions around it. If the buffalo were here today, I think they would be different from the buffalo of the old days because all the natural conditions have changed. They would not find the same food, nor the same surroundings. We see the change in our ponies. In the old days they could stand great hardship and travel long distance without water. They lived on certain kinds of food and drank pure water. Now our horses require a mixture of food; they have less endurance and must have constant care. It is the same with the Indians; they have less freedom and they fall an easy prey to disease. In the old days they were rugged and healthy, drinking pure water and eating the meat of the buffalo, which had a wide range, not being shut up like cattle of the present day. The water of the Missouri River is not pure, as it used to be, and many of the creeks are no longer good for us to drink.

A man ought to desire that which is genuine instead of that which is artificial. Long ago there was no such thing as a mixture of earths to make paint. There were only three colors of native earth paint — red, white, and black. These could be obtained only in certain places. When other colors were desired, the Indians mixed the juices of plants, but it was found that these mixed colors faded and it could always be told when the red was genuine — the red made of burned clay.

Navajo Shrine

N. Scott Momaday is a contemporary Kiowa Indian and a Pulitzer Prize winner. In the following passage he describes part of a pilgrimage he made to the grave of his Kiowa grandmother.

A SINGLE KNOLL RISES OUT OF THE PLAIN IN OKLAHOMA, north and west of the Wichita Range. For my people, the Kiowas, it is an old landmark, and they gave it the name Rainy Mountain. The hardest weather in the world is there. Winter brings blizzards, hot tornadic winds arise in the spring, and in the summer the prairie is an anvil's edge. The grass turns brittle and brown, and it cracks beneath your feet. There are green belts along the river and creeks, linear groves of hickory and pecan, willow and witch hazel. At a distance in July or August the steaming foliage seems almost to writhe in fire. Great green and yellow grasshoppers are everywhere in the tall grass, popping up like corn to sting the flesh, and tortoises crawl about on the red earth, going nowhere in the plenty of time. Loneliness is an aspect of the land. All things in the plain are isolated; there is no confusion of objects in the eye, but one hill or one tree or one man. To look upon that landscape in the early morning, with the sun at your back, is to lose the sense of proportion. Your imagination comes to life, and this, you think, is where Creation was begun.

The relation between death and nature is described by Bedagi, or Big Thunder, in early 1900. Bedagi was of the Wabanakis Nation, which was made up of five tribes — Passamaquoddy, Penobscot, Micmac, Maliseet, and a tribe now gone that lived on the Kennebec River.

THE GREAT SPIRIT IS OUR FATHER, BUT THE EARTH IS OUR mother. She nourishes us; that which we put into the ground she returns to us, and healing plants she gives us likewise. If we are wounded, we go to our mother and seek to lay the wounded part against her, to be healed. Animals too, do thus, they lay their wounds to the earth. When we go hunting, it is not our arrow that kills the moose however powerful be the bow; it is nature that kills him. The arrow sticks in his hide; and, like all living things the moose goes to our mother to be healed. He seeks to lay his wound against the earth, and thus he drives the arrow farther in. Meanwhile I follow. He is out of sight, but I put my ear to a tree in the forest, and that brings me the sound, and I hear when the moose makes his next leap, and I follow. The moose stops again for the pain of the arrow, and he rubs his side upon the earth and drives the arrow farther in. I follow always, listening now and then with my ear against a tree. Every time he stops to rub his side he drives the arrow farther in, till at last when he is nearly exhausted and I come up with him, the arrow may be driven clean through his body. . . .

Born on March 20, 1871, Tatanga Mani, or Walking Buffalo, was destined to become an emissary of peace on behalf of the Canadian government. A Stoney Indian, he spent his very earliest years in Morley, Alberta, but was soon adopted by a white missionary, John McDougall. He was educated in the white man's schools, but never gave up "studying nature." In his old age, he was asked by the government to make a world tour as a representative of the Indian people. In an address in London, England, at the age of 87, he said: "Hills are always more beautiful than stone buildings, you know. Living in a city is an artificial existence. Lots of people hardly ever feel real soil under their feet, see plants grow except in flower pots, or get far enough beyond the street light to catch the enchantment of a night sky studded with stars. When people live far from scenes of the Great Spirit's making, it's easy for them to forget his laws." Tatanga Mani died in 1967.

WE WERE LAWLESS PEOPLE, BUT WE WERE ON PRETTY GOOD terms with the Great Spirit, creator and ruler of all. You whites assumed we were savages. You didn't understand our prayers. You didn't try to understand. When we sang our praises to the sun or moon or wind, you said we were worshipping idols. Without understanding, you condemned us as lost souls just because our form of worship was different from yours.

We saw the Great Spirit's work in almost everything: sun, moon, trees, wind, and mountains. Sometimes we approached him through these things. Was that so bad? I think we have a true belief in the supreme being, a stronger faith than that of most whites who have called us pagans. . . . Indians living close to nature and nature's ruler are not living in darkness.

Did you know that trees talk? Well they do. They talk to each other, and they'll talk to you if you listen. Trouble is, white people don't listen. They never learned to listen to the Indians so I don't suppose they'll listen to other voices in nature. But I have learned a lot from trees: sometimes about the weather, sometimes about animals, sometimes about the Great Spirit.

Jicarilla

Every shaman, an Indian holy man, has his own particular song which he sings when calling up his helping spirits. This was the song of Uvavnuk, an Eskimo woman shaman, celebrating the joy of being moved by nature. "To the Indian," writes Natalie Curtis in *The Indian's Book,* "song is the breath of the spirit that consecrates the act of life."○

The great sea
Has sent me adrift
It moves me
As the weed in a great river
Earth and the great weather
Move me
Have carried me away
And move my inward parts with joy.

Apache Reaper

To us the ashes of our ancestors are sacred and their resting place is hallowed ground.

Chief Seattle, Chief of the Dwamish, upon surrendering his land to Governor Isaac Stevens in 1855

Addressing the government commissioners at Warner's Hot Springs at the turn of the century, Cecilio Blacktooth speaks about why her people would not surrender their land.

WE THANK YOU FOR COMING HERE TO TALK TO US IN A WAY we can understand. It is the first time anyone has done so. You ask us to think what place we like next best to this place, where we always lived. You see the graveyard out there? There are our fathers and our grandfathers. You see that Eagle-nest mountain and that Rabbit-hole mountain? When God made them, He gave us this place. We have always been here. We do not care for any other place. . . . We have always lived here. We would rather die here. Our fathers did. We cannot leave them. Our children were born here — How can we go away? If you give us the best place in the world, it is not so good for us as this. . . . This is our home . . . We cannot live anywhere else. We were born here and our fathers are buried here. . . . We want this place and not any other. . . .

There is no other place for us. We do not want you to buy any other place. If you will not buy this place, we will go into the mountains like quail, and die there, the old people, and the women and children. Let the Government be glad and proud. It can kill us. We do not fight. We do what it says. If we cannot live here, we want to go into the mountains and die. We do not want any other home.

In the hour of his death in 1871, Tu-eka-kas, the father of Chief Joseph of the Nez Perces, reminded his son never to sell the bones of his father. Chief Joseph describes the death.

MY FATHER SENT FOR ME. I SAW HE WAS DYING. I TOOK HIS hand in mine. He said: "My son, my body is returning to my mother earth, and my spirit is going very soon to see the Great Spirit Chief. When I am gone, think of your country. You are the chief of these people. They look to you to guide them. Always remember that your father never sold his country. You must stop your ears whenever you are asked to sign a treaty selling your home. A few years more, and white men will be all around you. They have their eyes on this land. My son, never forget my dying words. This country holds your father's body. Never sell the bones of your father and your mother." I pressed my father's hand and told him I would protect his grave with my life. My father smiled and passed away to the spirit-land.

I buried him in that beautiful valley of winding waters. I love that land more than all the rest of the world. A man who would not love his father's grave is worse than a wild animal.

hief Seattle surrendered his land, on which the city of Seattle is now located, in 1855 (in the Port Elliott Treaty) and thereby doomed his people to reservation confinement. Seattle was an Indian of Salishan stock, and was chief of the Dwamish tribe of the Pacific Northwest, occupants of the Puget Sound Region. At the signing of the treaty, he addressed Governor Isaac Stevens.

MY PEOPLE ARE FEW. THEY RESEMBLE THE SCATTERING TREES of a storm-swept plain. . . . There was a time when our people covered the land as the waves of a wind-ruffled sea cover its shell-paved floor, but that time long since passed away with the greatness of tribes that are now but a mournful memory. . . .

To us the ashes of our ancestors are sacred and their resting place is hallowed ground. You wander far from the graves of your ancestors and seemingly without regret. Your religion was written on tables of stone by the iron finger of your God so that you could not forget. The Red Man could never comprehend nor remember it. Our religion is the traditions of our ancestors — the dreams of our old men, given them in the solemn hours of night by the Great Spirit; and the visions of our sachems, and is written in the hearts of our people.

Your dead cease to love you and the land of their nativity as soon as they pass the portals of the tomb and wander away beyond the stars. They are soon forgotten and never return. Our dead never forget the beautiful world that gave them being. . . .

When the last Red Man shall have perished, and the memory of my tribe shall have become a myth among the white man, these shores will swarm with the invisible dead of my tribe, and when your childrens' children think themselves alone in the field, the store, the shop, or in the silence of the pathless woods, they will not be alone. . . . At night when the streets of your cities and villages are silent and you think them deserted, they will throng with the returning hosts that once filled them and still love this beautiful land. The White Man will never be alone.

Let him be just and deal kindly with my people, for the dead are not powerless. Dead — I say? There is no death. Only a change of worlds.

The following funeral speech is one reported by Jonathan Carver who travelled through the interior parts of North America between the years 1766 and 1768. Carver claims to have heard the speech directly from the Indians (perhaps the Naudowessies). Like most funeral orations, the speech praises the departed friend, but unlike others, does so in an unusually eloquent manner. The relatives are seated around the body, and each in turn harangues the deceased; if he has been a great warrior, one recounts his heroic actions.

YOU STILL SIT AMONG US, BROTHER, YOUR PERSON RETAINS its usual resemblance and continues similar to ours, without any visible deficiency except that it has lost the power of action. But whither is that breath flown, which a few hours ago sent up breath to the Great Spirit? Why are those lips silent, that lately delivered to us expressive and pleasing language? Why are those feet motionless that a short time ago were fleeter than the deer on yonder mountains? Why useless hang those arms that could climb the tallest tree, or draw the toughest bow? Alas! every part of that frame which we lately beheld with admiration and wonder, is now become as inanimate as it was three hundred winters ago. We will not, however, bemoan thee as if thou wast forever lost to us, or that thy name would be buried in oblivion; thy soul yet lives in the great country of Spirits, with those of thy nation that are gone before thee; and though we are left behind to perpetuate thy fame, we shall one day join thee. Actuated by the respect we bore thee whilst living, we now come to tender to thee the last act of kindness it is in our power to bestow: that thy body might not lie neglected on the plain, and become a prey to the beasts of the field, or the fowls of the air, we will take care to lay it with those of thy predecessors who are gone before thee; hoping at the same time, that thy spirit will feed with their spirits, and be ready to receive ours, when we also shall arrive at the great Country of Souls.

Flathead Child

William W. Warren was born in May 1825, the son of an Ojibway mother and a white father. His ancestry revealed that he was a descendant of Richard Warren, one of the "Mayflower" pilgrims who landed in Plymouth in 1620. As a child he was schooled in the Indian manner. In 1842 he married and moved to what is now Minnesota, where he was employed as a government interpreter. In 1851 he became a member of the House of Representatives at St. Paul. About that time he began to write for *The Minnesota Democrat* about Indian legends and folklore. Fascinated by the traditions and tales of the "old men," he spent hours visiting with them in remote places. They would also come to talk to him; a frequent visitor was the famous Chief of the Pillagers, Esh-ke-bug-e-coshe, or Flatmouth, who always referred to Warren as "grandson." Warren died at the early age of 28, just having completed a history of his nation, based upon Ojibway traditions and oral statements. The following passage describes the "happy hunting grounds" of his people.

WHEN AN OJIBWAY DIES, HIS BODY IS PLACED IN A GRAVE, generally in a sitting posture, facing the west. With the body are buried all the articles needed in life for a journey. If a man, his gun, blanket, kettle, fire steel, flint and moccasins; if a woman, her moccasins, axe, portage collar, blanket and kettle. The soul is supposed to start immediately after the death of the body, on a deep beaten path, which leads westward; the first object he comes to, in following this path, is the great Oda-e-min (Heart berry), or strawberry, which stands on the roadside like a huge rock, and from which he takes a handful and eats on his way. He travels on till he reaches a deep, rapid stream of water, over which lies the much dreaded Ko-go-gaup-o-gun, or rolling and sinking bridge; once safely over this as the traveller looks back it assumes the shape of a huge serpent swimming, twisting and untwisting its folds across the stream.

After camping out four nights, and travelling each day through a prairie country, the soul arrives in the land of spirits, where he finds his relatives accumulated since mankind was first created; all is rejoicing, singing and dancing; they live in a beautiful country interspersed with clear lakes and streams, forests and prairies, and abounding in fruit and game to repletion — in a word, abounding in all that the red man most covets in this life, and which conduces most to his happiness. It is that kind of paradise which he only by his manner of life on this earth, is fitted to enjoy.

Apache Baby

Before talking of holy things, we prepare ourselves by offerings . . . one will fill his pipe and hand it to the other who will light it and offer it to the sky and earth . . . they will smoke together . . . . Then will they be ready to talk.

Mato-Kuwapi, or Chased-By-Bears,
a Santee-Yanktonai Sioux

Ohiyesa, the Santee Dakota physician and author, speaks in 1911 about the manner in which his people worship.

IN THE LIFE OF THE INDIAN THERE WAS ONLY ONE INEVITABLE duty, — the duty of prayer — the daily recognition of the Unseen and Eternal. His daily devotions were more necessary to him than daily food. He wakes at daybreak, puts on his moccasins and steps down to the water's edge. Here he throws handfuls of clear, cold water into his face, or plunges in bodily. After the bath, he stands erect before the advancing dawn, facing the sun as it dances upon the horizon, and offers his unspoken orison. His mate may precede or follow him in his devotions, but never accompanies him. Each soul must meet the morning sun, the new sweet earth and the Great Silence alone!

Whenever, in the course of the daily hunt the red hunter comes upon a scene that is strikingly beautiful or sublime — a black thundercloud with the rainbow's glowing arch above the mountain, a white waterfall in the heart of a green gorge; a vast prairie tinged with the blood-red of sunset — he pauses for an instant in the attitude of worship. He sees no need for setting apart one day in seven as a holy day, since to him all days are God's.

This old Dakota wiseman explains the use of the varied forms of life in Indian worship just prior to 1890. The pursuit of unity in life is discernible throughout.°

EVERYTHING AS IT MOVES, NOW AND THEN, HERE AND THERE, MAKES stops. The bird as it flies stops in one place to make its nest, and in another to rest in its flight. A man when he goes forth stops when he wills. So the god has stopped. The sun, which is so bright and beautiful, is one place where he has stopped. The moon, the stars, the winds, he has been with. The trees, the animals, are all where he has stopped, and the Indian thinks of these places and sends his prayers there to reach the place where the god has stopped and win help and a blessing.

Piegan Sun Dance Encampment

Mato-Kuwapi, or Chased-By-Bears, a Santee-Yanktonai Sioux, talks about the sun dance and the Indian's understanding of Wakan tanka just before his death in 1915. Mato-Kuwapi had first participated in the dance in 1867, when at the age of 24 he had "spoken the vow" of a war party. On that occasion as well as at other sun dances he cut the arms of the men, suspended them to the pole or fastened the buffalo skulls to their flesh, according to the nature of their vows.

THE SUN DANCE IS SO SACRED TO US THAT WE DO NOT TALK of it often. . . . The cutting of the bodies in fulfillment of a Sun dance vow is different from the cutting of the flesh when people are in sorrow. A man's body is his own, and when he gives his body or his flesh he is giving the only thing which really belongs to him. . . . Thus, if a man says he will give a horse to Wakan tanka, he is only giving that which already belongs to him. I might give tobacco or other articles in the Sun dance, but if I have these and kept back the best no one would believe that I was in earnest. I must give something that I really value to show that my whole being goes with the lesser gifts; therefore I promise to give my body.

A child believes that only the action of someone who is unfriendly can cause pain, but in the Sun dance we acknowledge first the goodness of Wakan tanka, and then we suffer pain because of what he has done for us. To this day I have never joined a Christian Church. The old belief which I have always held is still with me.

When a man does a piece of work which is admired by all we say that it is wonderful; but when we see the changes of day and night, the sun, moon, and stars in the sky, and the changing seasons upon the earth, with their ripening fruits, anyone must realize that it is the work of some one more powerful than man. Greatest of all is the sun, without which we could not live. . . .

We talk to Wakan tanka and are sure he hears us, and yet it is hard to explain what we believe about this. It is the general belief of the Indians that after a man dies his spirit is somewhere on the earth or in the sky, we do not know exactly where but we are sure that his spirit still lives. Sometimes people have agreed together that if it were found possible for spirits to speak to men, they would make themselves known to their friends after they died, but they never came to speak to us again, unless, perhaps, in our sleeping dreams. So it is with Wakan tanka. We believe that he is everywhere, yet, he is to us as the spirits of our friends, whose voices we can not hear.

Every significant act in the daily life of the Kwakiutl, native of British Columbia, had a ritual and a prayer connected with it. Erna Gunther, in *Further Analysis of the First Salmon Ceremony,* gives an example: "The fisherman catches four silver salmon and the canoe-builder throws four chips behind the tree because the Kwakiutl, like the Tsimshian, have four as their ritual number. There is a very definite formula to these prayers. The animal or plant prayed to is called, 'Friend, Supernatural One.' It is thanked for giving of its substance. It is asked to keep illness and death from the devotee. The canoe-builder answers his prayer as does the wife of the salmon fisherman." The following passages, translations by Franz Boas, of material dating around 1900, suggest the pervasiveness of this ritualism, which often, as in the example from Gunther, is developed around the use of four elements.° The first passage begins with the statement of a canoe-builder who, having almost felled a tree, has taken four chips of wood and thrown one behind the foot of the tree. He says:

"O SUPERNATURAL ONE! NOW FOLLOW YOUR SUPERNATURAL POWER!" Throwing another, he says, "O friend! Now you see your leader, who says that you shall turn your head and fall there also." He throws a third chip and says, "O life-giver! Now you have seen which way your supernatural power went. Now go the same way." He throws the last one saying, "O friend, now you will go where your heartwood goes. You will lie on your face at the same place." After he says this he answers himself, saying, "Yes, I shall fall with my top there."

When a woman cuts the roots of a young cedar tree she prays, "Look at me, friend! I come to ask for your dress, for you have come to take pity on us; for there is nothing for which you can not be used, because it is your way that there is nothing for which we cannot use you, for you are really willing to give us your dress. I come to beg you for this, long life-maker, for I am going to make a basket for lily roots out of you. I pray, friend, not to feel angry with me on account of what I am going to do to you, and I beg you, friend, to tell your friends about what I ask of you. Take care, friend! Keep sickness away from me, so that I may not be killed by sickness or in war, O friend!"

Havasupai Home

Hehaka Sapa, or Black Elk, belonged to the Oglala division of the Teton Dakota, one of the most powerful branches of the Siouan family. He was born in "the Moon of the Popping Trees [December] on the little Powder River in the winter when the Four Crows were killed in 1863." Related to the great Chief, Crazy Horse, he had known Sitting Bull and Red Cloud and was well acquainted with the early days of his people when they had roamed the Plains; he was also present at the battle of Little Big Horn. Later on in life he travelled with Buffalo Bill to Italy, France and England, where he danced for Queen Victoria. Black Elk possessed unique spiritual power recognized by everyone and had been instructed in his youth in the sacred traditions of his people by the great priests. His father had been a medicine man; several of his brothers also. He spent his last days on the Pine Ridge Reservation in South Dakota. The following passage is taken from his autobiography which he dictated in 1930-31 to Flaming Rainbow. The configuration of the circle, referred to here by Black Elk and in the next several texts, had a fundamental place in Indian life.°

YOU HAVE NOTICED THAT EVERYTHING AN INDIAN DOES IS IN A circle, and that is because the Power of the World always works in circles, and everything tries to be round. In the old days when we were a strong and happy people, all our power came to us from the sacred hoop of the nation and so long as the hoop was unbroken the people flourished. The flowering tree was the living center of the hoop, and the circle of the four quarters nourished it. The east gave peace and light, the south gave warmth, the west gave rain, and the north with its cold and mighty wind gave strength and endurance. This knowledge came to us from the outer world with our religion. Everything the Power of the World does is done in a circle. The Sky is round and I have heard that the earth is round like a ball and so are all the stars. The Wind, in its greatest power, whirls. Birds make their nests in circles, for theirs is the same religion as ours. The sun comes forth and goes down again in a circle. The moon does the same, and both are round.

Even the seasons form a great circle in their changing, and always come back again to where they were. The life of a man is a circle from childhood to childhood and so it is in everything where power moves. Our tipis were round like the nests of birds and these were always set in a circle, the nation's hoop, a nest of many nests where the Great Spirit meant for us to hatch our children.

The Song of the Seer is sung and told here by Tatanka-Ptecila, or Short Bull, a holy man, prophet and medicine man. A Dakota Sioux, he was revered among his people as a great worker of miracles. He was also one of the first followers of Wovoka, who started the ghost dance religion. "Do not fight . . . you must not fight" was one of Wovoka's messages. Tatanka-Ptecila brought back to his people the messages and the dance. He also made the charmed "ghost shirts" which would protect the Indians from the white man's bullet. He was a great leader among his people.

THE TRIBE ALWAYS CAMPED IN A CIRCLE AND IN THE MIDDLE OF the circle was a place called Hocoka, the center.

Before the people set out to war, the prophet, or holy man, made a tipi for himself and sat in it alone, looking into the future and seeing in vision all that would befall. The people brought him offerings of gifts, and he made holy emblems and charms to protect them in battle.

Then, before sending out the scouts, the warriors assembled in the center of the camp and sat in a circle awaiting the prophet. He came forth, singing a holy song, and bestowed upon the warriors the charms that he had made, and told to every man his fate.

There is the song of prophecy that he sang. In the last part of the song, where now there are only the sounds of no meaning, he sang words which foretold to each warrior the fate that would befall him in the strife. This song is sung when the tribe is going to war, just before the scouts set out to find the enemy.

SONG OF THE SEER

In this circle
O ye warriors
Lo, I tell you
Each his future.
All shall be
As I now reveal it
In this circle;
Hear ye!

Arikara Medicine Fraternity—The Prayer

II THE HAIRY MAN FROM THE EAST

We did not think of the great open plains, the beautiful rolling hills, and winding streams with tangled growth, as "wild." Only to the white man was nature a "wilderness" and only to him was the land "infested" with "wild" animals and "savage" people. To us it was tame. Earth was bountiful and we were surrounded with the blessings of the Great Mystery. Not until the hairy man from the east came and with brutal frenzy heaped injustices upon us and the families we loved was it "wild" for us. When the very animals of the forest began fleeing from his approach, then it was that for us the "Wild West" began.

Chief Luther Standing Bear,
of the Oglala band of Sioux

Little Wolf, Cheyenne

I wish all to know that I do not propose to sell any part of my country, nor will I have the whites cutting our timber along the rivers, more especially the oak. I am particularly fond of the little groves of oak trees. I love to look at them, because they endure the wintry storm and the summer's heat, and — not unlike ourselves — seem to flourish by them.

Tatanka Yotanka, or Sitting Bull, Sioux warrior

Gaspesian (now Micmac) Indian chief, in 1676, criticizes a group of French captains in Nova Scotia for the great esteem in which they hold French civilization.

THOU REPROACHEST US VERY INAPPROPRIATELY, THAT OUR country is a little hell on earth in contrast with France, which thou comparest to a terrestrial paradise, inasmuch as it yields thee, so thou sayest, every kind of provision in abundance. Thou sayest of us also that we are the most miserable and most unhappy of all men, living without religion, without manners, without honor, without social order, and in a word, without any rules, like the beasts in our woods and forests, lacking bread, wine, and a thousand other comforts, which thou hast in superfluity in Europe. Well, my brother, if thou doest not yet know the real feelings which our Indians have towards thy Country and towards all thy nation, it is proper that I inform thee at once.

I beg thee now to believe that, all miserable as we seem in thy eyes, we consider ourselves nevertheless much happier than thou, in this that we are very content with the little that we have. . . . Thou deceivest thyselves greatly if thou thinkest to persuade us that thy country is better than ours. For if France, as thou sayest, is a little terrestrial paradise, art thou sensible to leave it? And why abandon wives, children, relatives, and friends? Why risk thy life and thy property every year? And why venture thyself with such risk in any season whatsoever, to the storms and tempests of the sea in order to come to a strange and barbarous country which thou considerest the poorest and least fortunate of the world. Besides, since we are wholly convinced of the contrary, we scarcely take the trouble to go to France because we fear with good reason, lest we find little satisfaction there, seeing in our own experience that those who are natives thereof leave it every year in order to enrich themselves on our shores. We believe, further, that you are also incomparably poorer than we, and that you are only simple journeymen, valets, servants, and slaves, all masters and Grand Captains

48

though you may appear, seeing that you glory in our old rags, and in our miserable suits of beaver which can no longer be of use to us, and that you find among us in the fishery for cod which you make in these parts, the wherewithall to comfort your misery and the poverty which oppress you. As to us, we find all our riches and all our conveniences among ourselves, without trouble, without exposing our lives to the dangers in which you find yourselves constantly through your long voyages. And whilst feeling compassion for you in the sweetness of our repose, we wonder at the anxieties and cares which you give yourselves, night and day, in order to load your ships. We see also that all your people live, as a rule, only upon cod which you catch among us. It is everlastingly nothing but cod — cod in the morning, cod at midday, cod at evening, and always cod, until things come to such a pass that if you wish some good morsels it is at our expense; and you are obliged to have recourse to the Indians, whom you despise so much, and to beg them to go a-hunting that you may be regaled. Now tell me this one little thing, if thou hast any sense, which of these two is the wisest and happiest: he who labors without ceasing and only obtains . . . with great trouble, enough to live on, or he who rests in comfort and finds all that he needs in the pleasure of hunting and fishing.

It is true that we have not always had the use of bread and of wine which your France produces; but, in fact, before the arrival of the French in these parts, did not the Gaspesians live much longer than now? And if we have not any longer among us any of those old men of a hundred and thirty to forty years, it is only because we are gradually adopting your manner of living, for experience is making it very plain that those of us live longest who, despising your bread, your wine, and your brandy, are content with their natural food of beaver, of moose, of waterfowl, and fish, in accord with the custom of our ancestors and of all the Gaspesian nation. Learn now, my brother once for all, because I must open to thee my heart: there is no Indian who does not consider himself infinitely more happy and more powerful than the French.

dario, a seventeenth-century Huron chief, was also known as Kondiaronk (his Huron name) and The Rat (so called by the French). He had a high reputation for bravery and sagacity, and played a prominent part in Frontenac's War (1689-1697) — a series of conflicts between the French and English, and between the French along with their Indian allies and the Iroquois. His skill in diplomacy and confederating the tribes made him an acclaimed peacemaker. He died in Montreal during an important peace conference in 1701. Adario travelled widely and said of his travels: "I have been in France, New York and Quebec, where I Study'd the Customs and Doctrines of the English and French." The following discourse took place between Adario and Baron de Lahontan, a Frenchman, explorer and Lord Lieutenant of the French colony at Placentia in Newfoundland. Lahontan has just explained to Adario that without punishing the wicked and rewarding the good, murder and robbery would spread everywhere, and the white man would soon be the most miserable people upon the earth. Adario, in turn, interprets his understanding of the white man's law.

NAY, YOU ARE MISERABLE ENOUGH ALREADY, AND INDEED I CAN'T see how you can be more such. What sort of Men must the *EUROPEANS* be? What Species of Creatures do they retain to? The *EUROPEANS,* who must be forc'd to do Good, and have no other Prompter for the avoiding of Evil than the fear of Punishment. If I ask'd thee, what a Man is, thou wouldst answer me, He's a *FRENCHMAN,* and yet I'll prove that your *MAN* is rather a *BEAVER.* For *MAN* is not intitled to that character upon the force of his walking upright upon two Legs, or of Reading and Writing, and showing a Thousand other Instances of his Industry. . . .

Who gave you all the Countries that you now inhabit, by what Right do you possess them? They always belonged to the *ALGONKINS* before. In earnest, my dear Brother, I'm sorry for thee from the bottom of my soul. Take my advice, and turn *HURON;* for I see plainly a vast difference between thy condition and mine. I am Master of my Condition and mine. I am Master of my own Body, I have the absolute disposal of my self, I do what I please, I am the first and the last of my Nation, I fear no Man, and I depend only upon the Great Spirit. Whereas, thy Body, as well as thy Soul, are doomed to a dependence upon thy great Captain, thy Vice-Roy disposes of thee, thou hast not the liberty of doing what thou hast a mind to; thou art afraid of Robbers, false Witnesses, Assassins, etc., and thou dependest upon an infinity of Persons whose Places have raised them above thee. Is it true or not?

Curly Chief, a Pawnee, relates one of the early contacts between his people and the Europeans, between 1800—1820.

I HEARD THAT LONG AGO THERE WAS A TIME WHEN THERE WERE NO people in this country except Indians. After that the people began to hear of men that had white skins; they had been seen far to the east. Before I was born they came out to our country and visited us. The man who came was from the Government. He wanted to make a treaty with us, and to give us presents, blankets, and guns, and flint and steel and knives.

The Head Chief told him that we needed none of these things. He said, "We have our buffalo and our corn. These things the Ruler gave to us, and they are all that we need. See this robe. This keeps me warm in winter. I need no blanket."

The white men had with them some cattle, and the Pawnee Chief said, "Lead out a heifer here on the prairie!" They led her out, and the Chief, stepping up to her, shot her through behind the shoulder with his arrow, and she fell down and died. Then the Chief said, "Will not my arrow kill? I do not need your guns." Then he took his stone knife and skinned the heifer, and cut off a piece of fat meat. When he had done this he said, "Why should I take your knives? The Ruler has given me something to cut with."

Then taking the fire sticks, he kindled a fire to roast the meat, and while it was cooking, he spoke again and said, "You see, my brother, that the Ruler has given us all that we need for killing meat, or for cultivating the ground. Now go back to the country from whence you came. We do not want your presents, and do not want you to come into our country."

Fisherman, Wishham

A chief of one of the principal bands of the northern Blackfeet, upon being asked by U.S. delegates for his signature to one of the first land treaties in his region of the Milk River, near the northern border of Montana and the Northwest Territories, responds with a rejection of the money values of the white man.

OUR LAND IS MORE VALUABLE THAN YOUR MONEY. IT WILL LAST forever. It will not even perish by the flames of fire. As long as the sun shines and the waters flow, this land will be here to give life to men and animals. We cannot sell the lives of men and animals; therefore we cannot sell this land. It was put here for us by the Great Spirit and we cannot sell it because it does not belong to us. You can count your money and burn it within the nod of a buffalo's head, but only the Great Spirit can count the grains of sand and the blades of grass of these plains. As a present to you, we will give you anything we have that you can take with you; but the land, never.

The proud tribe of the Nez Perce (Pierced Nose) Indians was led by a most remarkable man named Hin-mah-too-yah-lat-kekht — Thunder Travelling to Loftier Mountain Heights — or Chief Joseph, whose description of the death of his father was quoted in Section 1. His affection for the land out of which he came never ceased, and Chief Joseph was unremitting in his attempts to remain in the valleys and mountains of his birthplace. In this passage he makes clear (as he was always accustomed to do) his sentiments regarding ownership of the earth.

THE EARTH WAS CREATED BY THE ASSISTANCE OF THE SUN, AND IT should be left as it was. . . . The country was made without lines of demarcation, and it is no man's business to divide it. . . . I see the whites all over the country gaining wealth, and see their desire to give us lands which are worthless. . . . The earth and myself are of one mind. The measure of the land and the measure of our bodies are the same. Say to us if you can say it, that you were sent by the Creative Power to talk to us. Perhaps you think the Creator sent you here to dispose of us as you see fit. If I thought you were sent by the Creator I might be induced to think you had a right to dispose of me. Do not misunderstand me, but understand me fully with reference to my affection for the land. I never said the land was mine to do with it as I chose. The one who has the right to dispose of it is the one who has created it. I claim a right to live on my land, and accord you the privilege to live on yours.

Two Strike, Brulé

Smohalla, founder of the dreamer religion, was born about 1815 or 1820, and belonged to the Sokulk, a small tribe of Nez Perce Indians, centering about Priest Rapids on the Columbia River in eastern Washington. Smohalla distinguished himself as a warrior and began to preach about 1850. He consistently rejected the white man's civilization and its teachings. The dreamer religion was a return to native concepts, particularly those of the benign Earthmother, with dreams being the sole source of supernatural power.° The doctrine, some details of which are revealed in the following statement, attracted many adherents, with some of the most devoted "dreamers" being Chief Joseph and his Nez Perces.

MY YOUNG MEN SHALL NEVER WORK. MEN WHO WORK CANNOT dream; and wisdom comes to us in dreams.

You ask me to plow the ground. Shall I take a knife and tear my mother's breast? Then when I die she will not take me to her bosom to rest.

You ask me to dig for stone. Shall I dig under her skin for her bones? Then when I die I cannot enter her body to be born again.

You ask me to cut grass and make hay and sell it and be rich like white men. But how dare I cut off my mother's hair?

On June 17, 1744, the commissioners from Maryland and Virginia negotiated a treaty with the Indians of the Six Nations at Lancaster, Pennsylvania. The Indians were invited to send boys to William and Mary College. The next day they declined the offer as follows.

WE KNOW THAT YOU HIGHLY ESTEEM THE KIND OF LEARNING taught in those Colleges, and that the Maintenance of our young Men, while with you, would be very expensive to you. We are convinced, that you mean to do us Good by your Proposal; and we thank you heartily. But you, who are wise must know that different Nations have different Conceptions of things and you will therefore not take it amiss, if our Ideas of this kind of Education happen not to be the same as yours. We have had some Experience of it. Several of our young People were formerly brought up at the Colleges of the Northern Provinces: they were instructed in all your Sciences; but, when they came back to us, they were bad Runners, ignorant of every means of living in the woods . . . neither fit for Hunters, Warriors, nor Counsellors, they were totally good for nothing.

   We are, however, not the less oblig'd by your kind Offer, tho' we decline accepting it; and, to show our grateful Sense of it, if the Gentlemen of Virginia will send us a Dozen of their Sons, we will take Care of their Education, instruct them in all we know, and make Men of them.

On the Little Bighorn

Village of the Kalispel

Sa-go-ye-wat-ha, or Red Jacket, Seneca chief, and great orator of the Six Nations, was born near the present site of Geneva, New York, in 1750. In 1805, a young missionary named Cram was sent into the country of the Iroquois by the Evangelical Missonary Society of Massachusetts to "spread the Word." A council was held at Buffalo, New York, and Red Jacket made the following reply telling Cram why he did not wish to have the missionary stay with them. N.B. Wood, in *Lives of Famous Indian Chiefs*, recounts that after making his statement Red Jacket moved to shake hands with the missionary; Cram refused saying, "There was no fellowship between the religion of God and the Devil." According to Wood, the Indians smiled and retired peacefully.

FRIEND AND BROTHER: IT WAS THE WILL OF THE GREAT SPIRIT THAT we should meet together this day. He orders all things, and has given us a fine day for our council. He has taken his garment from before the sun and caused it to shine with brightness upon us. For all these things we thank the Great Ruler, and Him *ONLY!*

Brother, this council-fire was kindled by you. It was at your request that we came together at this time. We have listened with joy to what you have said. You requested us to speak our minds freely. This gives us great joy, for we now consider that we stand upright before you and can speak what we think. All have heard your voice and can speak to you as one mind. Our minds are agreed.

Brother listen to what we say. There was a time when our forefathers owned this great island. Their seat extended from the rising to the setting sun. The Great Spirit had made it for the use of the Indians. He had created the buffalo, the deer and other animals for food. He had made the bear and beaver. Their skins served us for clothing. He had scattered them over the country and taught us how to take them. He had caused the earth to produce corn for bread. All this he had done for his red children because he loved them. If we had some disputes about our hunting ground they were generally settled without the shedding of much blood. But an evil day came upon us. Your forefathers crossed the great water and landed upon this land. Their numbers were small. They found us friends and not enemies. They told us they had fled from their own country on account of wicked men and had come here to enjoy their religion. They asked for a small seat. We took pity on them and granted their request and they sat down amongst us. We gave them corn and meat; they gave us poison [rum] in return. . . .

Brothers, our seats were once large, and yours were small. You have now become a great people, and we have scarcely a place left to spread our blankets. You have got our country, but are not satisfied; you want to force your religion upon us.

Brother, continue to listen. You say that you are sent to instruct us how to worship the Great Spirit agreeable to his mind; and if we do not take hold of the religion which you white people teach, we shall be unhappy hereafter. You say that you are right, and we are lost. How do we know this to be true? We understand that your religion is written in a book. If it was intended for us as well as you, why has not the Great Spirit given to us — and not only to us, but to our forefathers — the knowledge of that book, with the means of understanding it rightly? We only know what you tell us about it. How shall we know when to believe, being so often deceived by the white people?

Brother, you say there is but one way to worship and serve the Great Spirit. If there is but one religion, why do you white people differ so much about it? Why not all agree, as you can all read the book?

Brother, we do not understand these things. We are told that your religion was given to your forefathers, and has been handed down from father to son. We also, have a religion which was given to our forefathers, and has been handed down to us, their children. We worship in that way. It teaches us to be thankful for all favors we receive; to love each other, and be united. We never quarrel about religion, because it is a matter which concerns each man and the Great Spirit.

Brother, we do not wish to destroy your religion or take it from you; we only want to enjoy our own.

Brother, we have been told that you have been preaching to the white people in this place. These people are our neighbors: We are acquainted with them. We will wait a little while and see what effect your preaching has upon them. If we find it does them good, makes them honest and less disposed to cheat Indians, we will consider again of what you have said.

Brother, you have now heard our talk and this is all we have to say at present. As we are going to part, we will come and take you by the hand, and hope the Great Spirit will protect you on your journey, and return you safely to your friends.

Red Cloud, Oglala

Red Jacket's hostility toward Christianity erupted on every occasion. Referring to the unwise missionary Cram, he once said: "The White people were not content with the wrongs they had done his people, but wanted to *cram* their doctrines down their throats." When asked by a gentleman in 1824, why he was so opposed to missionaries, he replied:

THEY DO US NO GOOD. IF THEY ARE NOT USEFUL TO THE WHITE people and do them no good, why do they send them among the Indians? If they are useful to the white people and do them good, why do they not keep them at home? They [the white men] are surely bad enough to need the labor of everyone who can make them better. These men [the missionaries] know we do not understand their religion. We cannot read their book — they tell us different stories about what it contains, and we believe they make the book talk to suit themselves. If we had no money, no land and no country to be cheated out of these black coats would not trouble themselves about our good hereafter. The Great Spirit will not punish us for what we do not know. He will do justice to his red children. These black coats talk to the Great Spirit, and ask for light that we may see as they do, when they are blind themselves and quarrel about the light that guides them. These things we do not understand, and the light which they give us makes the straight and plain path trod by our fathers, dark and dreary. The black coats tell us to work and raise corn; they do nothing themselves and would starve to death if someone did not feed them. All they do is to pray to the Great Spirit; but that will not make corn and potatoes grow; if it will why do they beg from us and from the white people. The red men knew nothing of trouble until it came from the white men; as soon as they crossed the great waters they wanted our country, and in return have always been ready to teach us to quarrel about their religion. Red Jacket can never be the friend of such men. If they [the Indians] were raised among white people, and learned to work and read as they do, it would only make their situation worse. . . . We are few and weak, but may for a long time be happy if we hold fast to our country, and the religion of our fathers.

Chief Flying Hawk, a Sioux Indian of the Oglala clan, was a nephew of Sitting Bull; his full brother was Kicking Bear, who had been a leader of the ghost dances. Flying Hawk was born "about full moon of March 1852," a few miles south of Rapid City. As a youth he took part in tribal wars with the Crows and the Piegans and at the age of 24 had fought alongside the great Chief Crazy Horse when Custer's command was wiped out on the Little Bighorn in 1876. He became a chief at the age of 32. Later Flying Hawk joined Buffalo Bill's Show, Colonel Miller's 101 Ranch Show and the Sells-Floto Circus, and travelled throughout the country with each of them. He died at Pine Ridge, South Dakota, in 1931. In his old age, he said:

THE TIPI IS MUCH BETTER TO LIVE IN; ALWAYS CLEAN, WARM IN winter, cool in summer; easy to move. The white man builds big house, cost much money, like big cage, shut out sun, can never move; always sick. Indians and animals know better how to live than white man; nobody can be in good health if he does not have all the time fresh air, sunshine and good water. If the Great Spirit wanted men to stay in one place he would make the world stand still; but He made it to always change, so birds and animals can move and always have green grass and ripe berries, sunlight to work and play, and night to sleep; summer for flowers to bloom, and winter for them to sleep; always changing; everything for good; nothing for nothing.

The white man does not obey the Great Spirit; that is why the Indians never could agree with him.

Piegan Encampment

Wahunsonacock, or Powhatan, was the ruling chief and practically the founder of the Powhatan Confederacy in Virginia at the period of the first English settlement. In 1607 he questions Captain John Smith at Werowocomoco, in Virginia.

I HAVE SEEN TWO GENERATIONS OF MY PEOPLE DIE. NOT A MAN OF the two generations is alive now but myself. I know the difference between peace and war better than any man in my country. I am now grown old, and must die soon; my authority must descend to my brothers, Opitchapan, Opechancanough and Catatough — then to my two sisters, and then to my two daughters. I wish them to know as much as I do, and that your love to them may be like mine to you. Why will you take by force what you may have quietly by love? Why will you destroy us who supply you with food? What can you get by war? We can hide our provisions and run into the woods; then you will starve for wronging your friends. Why are you jealous of us? We are unarmed, and willing to give you what you ask, if you come in a friendly manner, and not with swords and guns, as if to make war upon an enemy. I am not so simple as not to know that it is much better to eat good meat, sleep comfortably, live quietly with my wives and children, laugh and be merry with the English, and trade for their copper and hatchets, than to run away from them, and to lie cold in the woods, feed on acorns, roots and such trash, and be so hunted that I can neither eat nor sleep. In these wars, my men must sit up watching, and if a twig break, they all cry out, "Here comes Captain Smith!" So I must end my miserable life. Take away your guns and swords, the cause of all our jealousy, or you may all die in the same manner.

Crazy Horse was a mystic, and was "revered and feared by all." An Oglala Sioux chief, he scorned reservation life and took great delight in raiding expeditions against the Crows or the Mandan. When the Sioux went on the warpath in 1875 on account of both the occupancy by the whites of the Black Hills and other grievances, Crazy Horse and Sitting Bull were the leaders of the hostiles. Both bands of Crazy Horse and Sitting Bull united in 1876 and annihilated the troops of Custer. The following spring, pursued by General Miles to Bighorn Mountains, Crazy Horse was forced to surrender. He was placed under arrest in September 1877, for suspicion of stirring up trouble again, and was killed trying to escape.

Unlike most other famous Indian figures, no picture was ever obtained of Crazy Horse, whose reply to any request to photograph him was: "My friend, why should you wish to shorten my life by taking from me my shadow?" He always stood firmly opposed to the white man's ways. His view of white encroachments upon his people's land is summed up in the following statement.

WE DID NOT ASK YOU WHITE MEN TO COME HERE. THE GREAT SPIRIT gave us this country as a home. You had yours. We did not interfere with you. The Great Spirit gave us plenty of land to live on, and buffalo, deer, antelope and other game. But you have come here; you are taking my land from me; you are killing off our game, so it is hard for us to live. Now, you tell us to work for a living, but the Great Spirit did not make us to work, but to live by hunting. You white men can work if you want to. We do not interfere with you, and again you say, why do you not become civilized? We do not want your civilization! We would live as our fathers did, and their fathers before them.

Skokomish Mussel Gatherer

The great man wanted only a little, little land, on which to raise greens for his soup, just as much as a bullock's hide would cover. Here we first might have observed their deceitful spirit.

Delaware view, passed down
through the oral tradition,
of the first arrival of the
Dutch at Manhattan Island,
about 1609

Every year our white intruders become more greedy, exacting, oppressive, and overbearing. . . . Wants and oppressions are our lot. . . . Are we not being stripped day by day of the little that remains of our ancient liberty? . . . Unless every tribe unanimously combines to give a check to the ambition and avarice of the whites, they will soon conquer us apart and disunited, and we will be driven away from our native country and scattered as autumnal leaves before the wind.

Tecumseh, a Shawnee chief,
in a speech in 1812

Princess Angeline, daughter of Chief Seattle

Hehaka Sapa, or Black Elk, the great Sioux chief, over sixty and nearly blind, reflects upon the invasion, between 1863 and 1890, of his people's lands by the white man, and sadly recounts their treatment of the buffalo. The "Winter of the Hundred Slain," to which he refers, is the Fetterman Fight, commonly described as a "massacre" in which a Captain Fetterman and 81 men were wiped out on Peno Creek near Fort Phil Kearney, December 21, 1866.

I CAN REMEMBER THAT WINTER OF THE HUNDRED SLAIN (1866) AS A man may remember some bad dream he dreamed when he was little, but I can not tell just how much I heard when I was bigger and how much I understood when I was little. It is like some fearful thing in a fog, for it was a time when everything seemed troubled and afraid.

I had never seen a Wasichu [white man] then, and did not know what one looked like; but everyone was saying that the Wasichus were coming and that they were going to take our country and rub us all out and that we should all have to die fighting.

Once we were happy in our own country and we were seldom hungry, for then the two-leggeds and the four-leggeds lived together like relatives, and there was plenty for them and for us. But the Wasichus came, and they have made little islands for us and other little islands for the four-leggeds, and always these islands are becoming smaller, for around them surges the gnawing flood of the Wasichu; and it is dirty with lies and greed.

I was ten years old that winter, and that was the first time I ever saw a Wasichu. At first I thought they all looked sick, and I was afraid they might just begin to fight us any time, but I got used to them.

I can remember when the bison were so many that they could not be counted, but more and more Wasichus came to kill them until there were only heaps of bones scattered where they used to be. The Wasichus did not kill them to eat; they killed them for the metal that makes them crazy, and they took only the hides to sell. Sometimes they did not even take the hides, only the tongues; and I have heard that fire-boats came down the Missouri River loaded with dried bison tongues. You can see that the men who did this were crazy. Sometimes they did not even take the tongues; they just killed and killed because they liked to do that. When we hunted bison, we killed only what we needed.

A Winter Campaign, Apsaroke

The following words were spoken by Speckled Snake, an aged Creek more than 100 years old, in the year 1829, when President Andrew Jackson recommended that all the Creeks, Chickasaws, Cherokees, Choctaws and Seminoles leave their eastern homes and take themselves westward, out of the white man's way beyond the Mississippi.

BROTHERS! I HAVE LISTENED TO MANY TALKS FROM OUR GREAT father. When he first came over the wide waters, he was but a little man . . . very little. His legs were cramped by sitting long in his big boat, and he begged for a little land to light his fire on . . . But when the white man had warmed himself before the Indians' fire and filled himself with their hominy, he became very large. With a step he bestrode the mountains, and his feet covered the plains and the valleys. His hand grasped the eastern and the western sea, and his head rested on the moon. Then he became our Great Father. He loved his red children, and he said, "Get a little further, lest I tread on thee. . . ."

Brothers I have listened to a great many talks from our great father. But they always began and ended in this — "Get a little further; you are too near me."

The tribe now called the Mojave-Apaches, whose original home was in the Verde Valley of Arizona, were hostile to the American invasion of their land, as were the Apaches. In about 1874 they were conquered and placed on a reservation in San Carlos County, Arizona, with the Apaches, and from this association came the name. "On their removal to San Carlos County," writes Natalie Curtis in *The Indian's Book,* "these Indians were promised that if they would remain there peacefully and adopt the white man's ways, they should be allowed, when civilized, to return to their land, there to resume their life of agriculture. . . . The Indians faithfully kept their pledge, but after twenty-nine years . . . they found their land in the Verde Valley completely taken up by the white settlers." A private citizen came to their rescue and, continues Curtis, "obtained the power to buy for the Indians from the settlers a fertile tract of country in the Verde Valley. . . . On Christmas Day in 1903 the land was divided among them. That night the Indians gave a dance in honor of their 'Savior' and in thanksgiving for their land, they said:

'WE HAVE OUR HOMES; WE ARE MEN AGAIN.'"

Basket-maker, Achomawi

Chief Slow Bull, Oglala

This next passage is exemplary of Sitting Bull's eloquence, as he vigorously defends his own character and condemns that of the white man.

WHAT TREATY THAT THE WHITES HAVE KEPT HAS THE RED MAN broken? Not one. What treaty that the white man ever made with us have they kept? Not one. When I was a boy the Sioux owned the world; the sun rose and set on their land; they sent ten thousand men to battle. Where are the warriors today? Who slew them? Where are our lands? Who owns them? What white man can say I ever stole his land or a penny of his money? Yet, they say I am a thief. What white woman, however lonely, was ever captive or insulted by me? Yet they say I am a bad Indian. What white man has ever seen me drunk? Who has ever come to me hungry and unfed? Who has ever seen me beat my wives or abuse my children? What law have I broken? Is it wrong for me to love my own? Is it wicked for me because my skin is red? Because I am a Sioux; because I was born where my father lived; because I would die for my people and my country?

The following speech of the chiefs and warriors of the Ottawan and Chippewa tribes, was addressed to a Colonel Cadwell, superintendent of Indian Affairs, at Chenaille Ecarti, in Canada, August 3, 1815. The Indians subtly remind the white man of their broken promises.

FATHER, LISTEN,

To what your children now present are going to say; when you speak to them, they listen. We also expect that you will hear them and what they are going to say.

Listen,

I am now going to tell you what has been promised to our forefathers, by our father the English.

Listen,

You promised to our ancestors that when you had anything to say to us that you would tell us your mind, and that if we had anything to tell you, we should do the same thing. You promised that you would always be ready to give us your advice and put us in the right path, and the same thing with us in case of your going wrong.

Listen,

You told us that we were upon this island and we were Indians which you esteemed most partially. But now that our old chiefs are dead it appears now to all the Chiefs and Warriors here that their Father has forgotten his former promises.

Listen, Father,

The Promise you made to our forefathers was that we should never be in want of anything, that you had plenty and that we should always be supplied of our wants, that you have goods enough to cover all the trees in Upper Canada. Father, you have promised so much; you do not perform.

Father,

You promised us that the weather would be clear and that your children should have so much silver that when they looked at each other they would look as bright as the rising sun. Perhaps you think that we do not remember those promises you have made to our ancestors. You told us that if we would both sit down together that when you would get up we should see the silver under you. Your children wish to refresh your memory. They think you have forgotten the promises made there.

Father,

You see what you have promised us. Our father at Quebec sends us plenty of goods but we think they are lost after they get here; they are lost for the Indians but we think that some person profits by them . . . .

Listen my Father,

When at Quebec I saw those articles, I mentioned to our Great Father that we did not receive such goods in our country; perhaps it is some white mouse that runs away with these articles. I am sure it is not a Black Mouse . . . . Father the reason I speak is that when you came up from Quebec you made us the same promises — that you would not put anything in your pocket but that everything that came up for us should be given. . . .

This is all I have to say to you; it is the opinion of the Chiefs and Young Men here present. We merely wish to refresh the memory of our Father. . . .

Kutenai Rush Gatherer

Tah-gah-jute, or Logan, the Mingo, was a noted Cayuga chief, who was born at Shamokin, Pennsylvania, about 1725. He was well known for his friendships with the white men. In 1774 a number of Indians including some of Logan's relatives, were brutally massacred at the mouth of Yellow Creek by settlers on the Ohio, in retaliation, it was claimed, for the murder of white immigrants. Repudiating his former beliefs, Logan made war on the border settlements for some months. The uprising was suppressed, but Logan refused to attend the treaty meeting at Chillicothe; instead he sent this message defending his conduct.

I APPEAL TO ANY WHITE MAN TO SAY, IF HE EVER ENTERED LOGAN'S cabin hungry, and he gave him no meat; if ever he came cold and naked, and he clothed him not.

During the course of the last long and bloody war, Logan remained idle in his cabin, an advocate of peace. Such was my love for the whites, that my countrymen pointed at me as they passed and said, "Logan is the friend of the white man."

I had even thought to have lived with you, but for the injuries of one man, Colonel Cressap, who last spring, in cold blood, and unprovoked, murdered all the relatives of Logan, not even sparing my women and children.

There runs not a drop of my blood in the veins of any living creature. This called on me for revenge. I have sought; I have killed many; I have glutted my vengeance; for my country I rejoice at the beams of peace.

But do not harbor a thought that mine is the joy of fear. Logan never knew fear. He will not turn on his heel to save his life. Who is there to mourn for Logan? Not one!

The following words are those of Pachgantschilhilas, who was born in the first half of the eighteenth century, and who became the head warrior of all the Delawares residing then on the Miami and White rivers, in the Northeastern United States. In the course of this address to the Moravian Indians in Ohio — these were Indians who had been converted by Moravian Missionaries and were then separated from their tribes — he tried to persuade them to remove themselves from their village in which they were vulnerable to attacks from the white frontiersmen, and move to a safer place. The source of this address, John Heckewelder, in *Account of the History, Manners, and Customs of the Indian Nations,* comments: "Eleven months after this speech was delivered by this prophetic chief, ninety-six of the same Christian Indians, about sixty of them women and children, were murdered at the place where these very words had been spoken, by the same men he had alluded to and in the same manner that he had described."

I ADMIT THAT THERE ARE GOOD WHITE MEN, BUT THEY BEAR NO proportion to the bad; the bad must be the strongest, for they rule. They do what they please. They enslave those who are not of their color, although created by the same Great Spirit who created us. They would make slaves of us if they could, but as they cannot do it, they kill us! There is no faith to be placed in their words. They are not like the Indians who are only enemies while at war and are friends in peace. They will say to an Indian, "my friend! my brother!" They will take him by the hand, and at the same moment destroy him. And so you, addressing himself to the Christian Indians, will also be treated by them before long. Remember! that this day I have warned you to beware of such friends as these. I know the *long knives;* they are not to be trusted.

"The prime cause for the westward migration of the Delaware and Shawnee from the Susquehanna to the Ohio," writes George P. Donehoo in *Carlisle and the Red Men of Other Days,* "was the debauchery caused by the rum traffic of the white Indian trader. Again and again wise chiefs of these tribes made complaint against this traffic, which was robbing their hunters of their furs and peltries, their warriors of their manhood and their women of their virtue." But the rum continued to flow and penetrated most Indian villages. Chiefs consistently objected to the sale of rum which they considered to be the white man's most awful curse. Their objections were in vain. Traders steadily grew wealthy and Indians began to live dissipated lives.

In an attempt to stop the white Indian traders from debauching his people, Scarouady, an Oneida chieftain and firm friend of the English colonists, made a speech at the first Indian council at Carlisle, Pennsylvania, September 28 to October 4, 1753.

WE DESIRE THAT PENNSYLVANIA AND VIRGINIA SHOULD FORBEAR settling our lands over the Alleghany hills. We advise you rather to call your people back to this side of the hills lest damage be done and you think ill of us. . . . Your traders now bring little powder and lead or other valuable goods. The rum ruins us. We beg you would prevent its coming in such quantities by regulating the traders. When these whisky traders come they bring thirty or forty caggs [kegs] and put them down before us and make us drunk, and get all the skins that should go to pay the debts we have contracted for goods bought of the fair traders, and by this means we not only ruin ourselves but them [the fair traders] too. These wicked whisky sellers, when they have once got the Indians in liquor, make them sell their very clothes from their backs. In short, if this practice be continued we must inevitably be ruined.

Jack Red Cloud, son of Chief Red Cloud, Oglala

Tecumseh, or Shooting Star, was a celebrated Shawnee war chief, and an ardent opponent of the white man's advances. He was the leading Shawnee orator; according to an Indian biographer, "the Indians were raised to a perfect frenzy by his fiery eloquence." Tecumseh organized the second great Indian confederation and was made a brigadier general in the British Army in the War of 1812.

In a treaty at Fort Wayne in 1809, the Indians ceded to the American government a large tract of land without Tecumseh's knowledge. On August 12, 1810, Tecumseh met at Vincennes with General W.H. Harrison, governor of Indiana Territory, who had represented the United States at the 1809 treaty. Tecumseh repudiated the validity of the land purchase.

I AM A SHAWNEE. MY FOREFATHERS WERE WARRIORS. THEIR SON IS a warrior. From them I take only my existence, from my tribe I take nothing. I am the maker of my own fortune, and Oh! that I could make that of my Red people, and of my country, as great as the conceptions of my mind, when I think of the Spirit that rules the universe. I would not then come to Governor Harrison to ask him to tear up the treaty [of 1809] , and to obliterate the landmark, but I would say to him: "Sir, you have liberty to return to your own country."

The Being within, communing with past ages, tells me that once, nor until lately, there was no Whiteman on this continent, that it then all belonged to the Great Spirit that made them to keep it, to traverse it, to enjoy its productions, and to fill it with the same race, once a happy race; since made miserable by the White people, who are never contented but always encroaching.

The way, and the only way, to check and to stop this evil, is for all the Redmen to unite in claiming a common and equal right in the land, as it was at first and should be yet; for it was never divided, but belongs to all for the use of each. That no part has a right to sell, even to each other, much less to strangers — those who want all and will not do with less. The White people have no right to take the land from the Indians, because they had it first, it is theirs.... There cannot be two occupations in the same place. The first excludes all others. It is not so in hunting or travelling, for there the same ground will serve many . . . but the camp is stationary. . . . It belongs to the first who sits down on his blanket or skins, which he has thrown upon the ground, and till he leaves it, no other has a right.

Sioux Woman

At the great Indian council of October 1811, the Shawnees came down from the north and gathered along with about 5,000 others at Tukabatchi, on the west bank of Tallapoosa River in Alabama. It was here that Tecumseh, enraged by continual white encroachments, began his call to vengeance against the white man.

ACCURSED BE THE RACE THAT HAS SEIZED ON OUR COUNTRY AND made women of our warriors. Our fathers from their tombs reproach us as slaves and cowards. I hear them now in the wailing winds . . . the spirits of the mighty dead complain. Their tears drop from the wailing skies. Let the white race perish. They seize your land, they corrupt your women, they trample on the ashes of your dead! Back whence they came, upon a trail of blood, they must be driven.

Roman Nose was a noted warrior and intrepid chief of the southern Cheyennes. Between 1864 and 1870 as white settlers began to push into the sacred territory of the Cheyennes, Roman Nose and his band swept the Kansas frontier in revenge, attacking white homesteads and fighting the railway gangs who were laying the tracks for the Kansas Pacific Railroad. Early in this period, at a council in 1866, near Fort Ellsworth, Kansas, held between General Palmer and the chiefs of the Cheyenne tribe, Roman Nose protested the white invasion of their soil.

WE WILL NOT HAVE THE WAGONS WHICH MAKE A NOISE [STEAM engines] in the hunting grounds of the buffalo. If the palefaces come farther into our land, there will be scalps of your brethren in the wigwams of the Cheyennes. I have spoken.

Fish Shows, Apsaroke

Tatanka Yotanka, or Sitting Bull, Sioux warrior, tribal leader of the Hunkpapa Teton division and in later life a sacred "dreamer," was on the warpath almost continuously from 1869 to 1876. White settlers were pouring into the land, and even more disastrously for the Indians, gold had been discovered in the Black Hills country. Following this discovery, the government in 1875 ordered the Sioux to leave their Powder River hunting grounds, land which had been guaranteed to them in the treaty of 1868. The war of 1876 was fought to enforce the government's order. At a Powder River council in 1877, Sitting Bull expressed his great love for his native soil, "a love wholly mystical," writes a biographer of Sitting Bull. "He used to say [that] healthy feet can hear the very heart of Holy Earth. . . . Up always before dawn, he liked to bathe his bare feet, walking about in the morning dew."

BEHOLD, MY BROTHERS, THE SPRING HAS COME; THE EARTH HAS received the embraces of the sun and we shall soon see the results of that love!

Every seed is awakened and so has all animal life. It is through this mysterious power that we too have our being and we therefore yield to our neighbors, even our animal neighbors, the same right as ourselves, to inhabit this land.

Yet, hear me, people, we have now to deal with another race — small and feeble when our fathers first met them but now great and overbearing. Strangely enough they have a mind to till the soil and the love of possession is a disease with them. These people have made many rules that the rich may break but the poor may not. They take tithes from the poor and weak to support the rich who rule. They claim this mother of ours, the earth, for their own and fence their neighbors away; they deface her with their buildings and their refuse. That nation is like a spring freshet that overruns its banks and destroys all who are in its path.

We cannot dwell side by side. Only seven years ago we made a treaty by which we were assured that the buffalo country should be left to us forever. Now they threaten to take that away from us. My brothers, shall we submit or shall we say to them: "First kill me before you take possession of my Fatherland. . . ."

Sitting Bull consistently refused to submit to reservation life. "God made me an Indian," he would say, "but not a reservation Indian." After the battle on Little Big-horn in 1876, Sitting Bull fled to Canada where he was allowed to live in peace. The circumstance of a "renegade" American Indian being treated well in Canada was a constant source of embarrassment to the American government. Finally, an American commission led by General Alfred Terry came to Canada to entreat Sitting Bull and his small band of Sioux to return to the United States and agency life. Sitting Bull replied to General Terry's request by first reviewing all his tribe's experiences with the Great White Father, reminding him of the innumerable broken treaties and promises, and then he continued:

FOR 64 YEARS YOU HAVE PERSECUTED MY PEOPLE. I ASK YOU WHAT we have done to cause us to depart from our own country? I will tell you. We had no place to go, so we took refuge here. It was on this side of the boundary I first learned to shoot and be a man. For that reason I have come back. I was kept ever on the move until I was compelled to foresake my own lands and come here. I was raised close to, and today shake hands with, these people. [He strides toward Canadian Commissioner Macleod and Superintendent Walsh, shakes hands with them, then turns to the American commissioners.]

That is the way I came to know these people, and that is the way I propose to live. We did not give you our country; you took it from us. Look how I stand with these people [pointing to the Canadian North West Mounted Police]. Look at me. You think I am a fool, but you are a greater fool than I am. This house, the home of the English, is a medicine house [the abode of truth] and you come here to tell us lies. We do not want to hear them. Now I have said enough. You can go back. Say no more. Take your lies with you. I will stay with these people. The country we came from belonged to us; you took it from us; we will live here.

Big Bear, one of the great Indians of Canadian history, was a Cree Indian, a native of the Carlton district. He was first recognized as a chief upon the occasion of treaty #6 (sixth of the eleven post-confederation treaties in Canada), when he led a small group of stubborn Indians who refused to sign away the territorial rights of their forefathers. He was unwilling to accept the fact that the days of his people's untrammelled freedom were numbered. At the council at Duck Lake in Canada, July 31, 1884, Big Bear pleaded for united Indian action and denounced the whites for their lack of good faith.

I HAVE BEEN TRYING TO SEIZE THE PROMISES WHICH THEY [THE whites] made to me; I have been grasping but I cannot find them. What they have promised me straight way, I have not yet seen the half of it.

We have all been deceived in the same way. It is the cause of our meeting at Duck Lake. They offered me a spot as a reserve. As I see that they are not going to be honest, I am afraid to take a reserve. They have given me to choose between several small reserves but I feel sad to abandon the liberty of my own land when they come to me and offer me small plots to stay there and in return not to get half of what they have promised me. When will you have a big meeting? It has come to me as through the bushes that you are not yet all united; take time and become united, and I will speak. The Government sent to us those who think themselves men. They are not men. They have no honesty. They are an unsightly beast. Their faces are twisted from the appearance of honest men.

White Calf, Piegan

Mahpiua Luta, or Red Cloud, a principal chief of the Oglala Sioux, was born at the fork of the Platte River, Nebraska, in 1822. Throughout his life he fought every attempt of the whites to drive a road through Powder River country to the gold regions of Montana. A treaty in 1851 gave the whites the right to pass through Indian territory. They proceeded to disregard the treaty by building forts and attempting to open roads. In 1866, at a council at Fort Laramie, Wyoming, Red Cloud repeated his refusal to endanger the hunting grounds of his people, and angered by the lack of good faith of the whites, defiantly addressed his people.

HEAR YE, DAKOTAS! WHEN THE GREAT FATHER AT WASHINGTON sent us his chief soldier [Major General William S. Harney] to ask for a path through our hunting grounds, a way for his iron road to the mountains and the western sea, we were told that they wished merely to pass through our country, not to tarry among us, but to seek for gold in the far west. Our old chiefs thought to show their friendship and good will, when they allowed this dangerous snake in our midst. . . .

Yet before the ashes of the council fire are cold, the Great Father is building his forts among us. You have heard the sound of the white soldier's axe upon the Little Piney. His presence here is an insult and a threat. It is an insult to the spirits of our ancestors. Are we then to give up their sacred graves to be plowed for corn? Dakotas, I am for war!

Oglala Woman

The Dawes Commission, established by the United States government to investigate Indian life among the Choctaws and Chickasaws, recommended that the tribal governments of both nations be torn down, their lands be allotted and a territorial government established over them, and the people be made citizens of the United States. Some of the reasons given varied from "tribal governments afford no protection to human life" to the assertions that valuable coal mines on the land were being monopolized by a few individuals and that many white children were being reared in ignorance in Indian territory for want of education facilities. On this last point, the Indians replied that the country belonged to them and not the white man. "We have long since surrendered our surplus [land]," they said "to the Government to make homes for the white man. . . . A large part of the consideration for the surrender was the solemn guarantee of the United States, by treaty, that the foot of the white man should never invade our new homes, and that no Territorial or State Government should ever be extended over us, without our consent. And now we are met with the argument that so many white people are domiciled in our country [and] . . . in order to protect them, we must consent to have our tribal Governments broken up, our lands allotted and a Territorial Government established over us!"

The following answer to the Dawes Commission Report is addressed to the President of the United States and the Senate and the House of Representatives, by the delegates of the Choctaw and Chickasaw Nation in Indian territory, about 1895.

WE DESIRE TO RECALL A LITTLE HISTORY OF OUR PEOPLE. THE Choctaw and Chickasaw people have never cost the United States a cent for support. They have always and are now self-sustaining. It will be admitted that but little over a half a century ago the Choctaws and Chickasaws were happily located east of the Mississippi River. Their possessions were large and rich and valuable. The whites began to crowd around and among us in the east, as they now are in the west. The Government of the United States urged us to relinquish our valuable possessions there to make homes for their own people and to accept new reservations west of the great river Mississippi, assuring us that there we would be secure from the invasion of the white man. Upon condition that the Government would protect us from such renewed invasion and would give us the lands in fee and convey them to us by patent, and would, by solemn treaty guarantee that no Territorial or State Government should ever be extended over us without consent, and as it was to yield up and surrender our old homes, we consented, and with heavy hearts we turned our backs upon the graves of our fathers and took up the dismal march for our new western home, in a wilderness west of the Mississippi River. After long and tedious marches, after suffering great exposure and much loss of life, we reached the new reservation, with but one consolation to revive our drooping spirits, which was that we were never again to be molested. There, in the jungle and wilds, with nothing but wild animals and beasts for neighbors, we went to work in our crude way to build homes and Governments suited to our people.

In 1855, at the request of the United States we leased and sold the entire west part of our reservation amounting to over 12 million acres, for the purpose of homes for the white man and of locating thereon other friendly Indians. Again in 1866, at the urgent request of the Government we gave up all that part leased for the occupancy of friendly Indians, and ceded it absolutely for the same purpose. And again, in 1890 and 1891, we relinquished . . . 3 million acres . . . to be occupied by the whites. Now in less than five years we are asked to surrender completely our tribal governments and to accept a Territorial Government in lieu thereof; to allot our lands in severalty, and to become citizens of the United States and what is worse, an effort is being made to force us to do so against our consent. Such a radical change would, in our judgement, in a few years annihilate the Indian. . . .

We ask every lover of justice, is it right that a great and powerful government should, year by year, continue to demand cessions of land from weaker and dependent people, under the plea of securing homes for the homeless. While the great government of the United States, our guardian, is year by year admitting foreign paupers into the Union, at the rate of 250,000 per annum, must we sacrifice our homes and children for this pauper element?

We have lived with our people all our lives and believe that we know more about them than any Commission, however good and intelligent, could know from a few visits . . . on the railroads and towns, where but a few Indians are to be seen and where but few live. . . . They [the white man] care nothing for the fate of the Indian, so that their own greed can be gratified.

Crow Eagle, Piegan

The man who sat on the ground in his tipi meditating on life and its meaning, accepting the kinship of all creatures and acknowledging unity with the universe of things was infusing into his being the true essence of civilization. And when native man left off this form of development, his humanization was retarded in growth.

Chief Luther Standing Bear

In May 1847 the paper, "Territorial Limits, Geographical Names and Trails of the Iroquois," was delivered at a meeting of the New York Historical Society. Wa-o-wo-wa-no-onk (Dr. Peter Wilson), an educated Cayuga chief was present and made the following comments in response to the statement that "the Iroquois had left no monuments."

THAT LAND OF GANONO-O OR 'EMPIRE STATE' AS YOU LOVE TO CALL it was once laced by our trails from Albany to Buffalo — trails that we had trod for centuries — trails worn so deep by the feet of the Iroquois that they became your own roads of travel as your possessions gradually eat into those of my people. Your roads still traverse those same lines of communication and bind one part of the Long House to another. The land of Ganono-o, the Empire State, then is our monument! We shall not long occupy much room in living; the single tree of the thousands which sheltered our forefathers — one old elm under which the representatives of the tribes were wont to meet — will cover us all; but we would have our bodies twined in death among its roots, on the very soil on whence it grew! Perhaps it will last no longer being fertilized by their decay. . . .

In your last war with England, your red brother — your elder brother — still came up to help you as of old on the Canada frontier! Have we, the first holders of this prosperous region, no longer a share in your history? Glad were your fathers to sit upon the threshold of the Long House, rich did they then hold themselves in getting the mere sweeping from its door.

Had our forefathers spurned you from it when the French were thundering at the opposite end to get a passage through and drive you into the sea? Whatever has been the fate of other Indians, the Iroquois might still have been a nation; and I instead of pleading for the privilege of living within your borders — I — I might have had a country!

Sioux Winter Camp

Born in the summer of 1848 near the present site of Billings, Montana, Plenty-Coups, or Aleek-chea-ahoosh — Many Achievements — received his name from his grandfather who said "I have dreamed that he shall live to count many coups and be old; my dream also told me that he shall be a chief — the greatest chief our people will ever have," a prophecy that was later realized. Plenty-Coups died in 1932, shortly after willing to the American people his land of 200 acres (located in a valley in south-eastern Montana) to be a park as "a memorial to the Crow Nation" and "a token of my friendship for all people, both red and white." At his request, he was buried at the back of his house in the grove of cottonwood which he had planted as a young man. The following is an extract from his autobiography.

BY THE TIME I WAS FORTY, I COULD SEE OUR COUNTRY WAS changing fast, and that these changes were causing us to live very differently. Anybody could now see that soon there would be no buffalo on the plains and everybody was wondering how we could live after they were gone. There were few war parties, and almost no raids. . . . White men with their spotted-buffalo [cattle] were on the plains about us. Their houses were near the water-holes, and their villages on the rivers. We made up our minds to be friendly with them, in spite of all the changes they were bringing. But we found this difficult, because the white men too often promised to do one thing and then when they acted at all, did another.

They spoke very loudly when they said their laws were made for everybody; but we soon learned that although they expected us to keep them, they thought nothing of breaking them themselves. They told us not to drink whisky, yet they made it themselves and traded it to us for furs and robes until both were nearly gone. Their Wise Ones said we might have their religion, but when we tried to understand it we found that there were too many kinds of religion among white men for us to understand, and that scarcely any two white men agreed which was the right one to learn. This bothered us a good deal until we saw that the white man did not take his religion any more seriously than he did his laws, and that he kept both of them just behind him, like Helpers, to use when they might do him good in his dealings with strangers. These were not our ways. We kept the laws we made and lived our religion. We have never been able to understand the white man, who fools nobody but himself.

As a child, Chief Luther Standing Bear attended the white man's school at Carlisle. "I remember when we children were on our way to Carlisle School, thinking that we were on our way to meet death at the hands of the white people, the older boys sang brave songs, so that we would all meet death according to the code of the Lakota — fearlessly.... The brave song was to fortify one to meet any ordeal bravely and to keep up faltering spirits." Here, in a passage from his autobiography, *Land of the Spotted Eagle,* he talks about that experience and about some of the most ordinary customs of the white man that were offensive or deleterious to the Indian.

THE CLOTHING OF THE WHITE MAN, ADOPTED BY THE LAKOTA, HAD much to do with the physical welfare of the tribe, and at Carlisle School where the change from tribal to white man's clothing was sudden and direct, the effect on the health and comfort of the children was considerable. Our first resentment was in having our hair cut. It has ever been the custom of Lakota men to wear long hair, and old tribal members still wear the hair in this manner. On first hearing the rule, some of the older boys talked of resisting, but realizing the uselessness of doing so, submitted. But for days after being shorn we felt strange and uncomfortable. If the argument that has been advanced is true, that the children needed delousing, then why were not girls as well as boys put through the same process? The fact is that we were to be transformed, and short hair being the mark of gentility with the white man, he put upon us the mark, though he still retained his own custom of keeping the hair-covering on his face.

Our second resentment was against trousers, based upon what we considered the best of hygienic reasons. Our bodies were used to constant bathing in the sun, air, and rain, and the function of the pores of our skin, which were in reality a highly developed breathing apparatus, was at once stopped by trousers of heavy, sweat-absorbing material aided by that worst of all torments — red flannel underwear. For the stiff collars, stiff-front shirts, and derby hats no word of praise is due, and the heavy, squeaky, leather boots were positive tormentors which we endured because we thought that when we wore them we were "dressed up." Many times we have been laughed at for our native way of dressing, but could anything we ever wore compare in utter foolishness to the steel-ribbed corset and the huge bustle which our girls adopted after a few years in school?

Certain small ways and observances sometimes have connection with larger and more profound ideas, and for reasons of this sort the Lakota disliked the pocket handkerchief and found the white man's use of this toilet article very distasteful. The Indian, essentially an outdoor person, had no use for the handkerchief; he was practically immune to colds, and like the animal, not addicted to spitting. The white man, essentially an indoor person, was subject to colds, catarrh, bronchitis, and kindred diseases. He was a cougher and a spitter, and his constant use of tobacco aggravated the habit. With him the handkerchief was a toilet necessity. So it is easy to see why the Indian considered the carrying of a handkerchief an uncleanly habit.

According to the white man, the Indian, choosing to return to his tribal manners and dress, "goes back to the blanket." True, but "going back to the blanket" is the factor that has saved him from, or at least stayed, his final destruction. Had the Indian been as completely subdued in spirit as he was in body he would have perished within the century of his subjection. But is it the unquenchable spirit that has saved him — his clinging to Indian ways, Indian thought, and tradition, that has kept him and is keeping him today. The white man's ways were not his ways and many of the things that he has tried to adopt have proven disastrous and to his utter shame. Could the Indian have forestalled the flattery and deceit of his European subjector and retained his native truth and honesty; could he have shunned whiskey and disease and remained the paragon of health and strength he was, he might today be a recognized man instead of a hostage on a reservation. But many an Indian has accomplished his own personal salvation by "going back to the blanket." The Indian blanket or buffalo robe, a true American garment, and worn with the significance of language, covered beneath it, in the prototype of the American Indian, one of the bravest attempts ever made by man on this continent to rise to heights of true humanity.

To clothe a man falsely is only to distress his spirit and to make him incongruous and ridiculous, and my entreaty to the American Indian is to retain his tribal dress.

Cheyenne

Tatanga Mani, a Stoney Indian, in a passage from his autobiography, comments on the white man's education that he received.

OH, YES, I WENT TO THE WHITE MAN'S SCHOOLS. I LEARNED TO READ from school books, newspapers, and the Bible. But in time I found that these were not enough. Civilized people depend too much on man-made printed pages. I turn to the Great Spirit's book which is the whole of his creation. You can read a big part of that book if you study nature. You know, if you take all your books, lay them out under the sun, and let the snow and rain and insects work on them for a while, there will be nothing left. But the Great Spirit has provided you and me with an opportunity for study in nature's university, the forests, the rivers, the mountains, and the animals which include us.

This statement comes from Chief Luther Standing Bear's autobiography published in 1933.

THE WHITE MAN DOES NOT UNDERSTAND THE INDIAN FOR THE reason that he does not understand America. He is too far removed from its formative processes. The roots of the tree of his life have not yet grasped the rock and soil. The white man is still troubled with primitive fears; he still has in his consciousness the perils of this frontier continent, some of its vastnesses not yet having yielded to his questing footsteps and inquiring eyes. He shudders still with the memory of the loss of his forefathers upon its scorching deserts and forbidding mountain-tops. The man from Europe is still a foreigner and an alien. And he still hates the man who questioned his path across the continent. But in the Indian the spirit of the land is still vested; it will be until other men are able to divine and meet its rhythm. Men must be born and reborn to belong. Their bodies must be formed of the dust of their forefather's bones.

Born in March 1890, Sun Chief grew up among the Hopi in Oraibi, Arizona. In his youth, he attended the Sherman Institute in Riverside, California, where he acquired a good knowledge of English and adapted quickly to the white man's ways. However, he later returned to live with his people in Oraibi. Between 1938 and 1941 he wrote the story of his life; the following extract is a comment on his early experiences.

I HAD LEARNED MANY ENGLISH WORDS AND COULD RECITE PART OF the Ten Commandments. I knew how to sleep on a bed, pray to Jesus, comb my hair, eat with a knife and fork, and use a toilet. . . . I had also learned that a person thinks with his head instead of his heart.

Red Wing, Apsaroke

Ohiyesa, the celebrated writer, looks back over the past.

AS A CHILD I UNDERSTOOD HOW TO GIVE; I HAVE FORGOTTEN THIS grace since I became civilized. I lived the natural life, whereas I now live the artificial. Any pretty pebble was valuable to me then; every growing tree an object of reverence. Now I worship with the white man before a painted landscape whose value is estimated in dollars! Thus the Indian is reconstructed, as the natural rocks are ground to powder and made into artificial blocks which may be built into the walls of modern society.

The first American mingled with his pride a singular humility. Spiritual arrogance was foreign to his nature and teaching. He never claimed that the power of articulate speech was proof of superiority over the dumb creation; on the other hand, it is to him a perilous gift. He believes profoundly in silence — the sign of a perfect equilibrium. Silence is the absolute poise or balance of body, mind and spirit. The man who preserves his selfhood is ever calm and unshaken by the storms of existence — not a leaf, as it were, astir on the tree; not a ripple upon the surface of the shining pool — his, in the mind of the unlettered sage, is the ideal attitude and conduct of life.

If you ask him: "What is silence?" he will answer: "It is the Great Mystery!" "The holy silence is His voice!" If you ask: "What are the fruits of silence?" he will say: "They are self-control, true courage or endurance, patience, dignity, and reverence. Silence is the cornerstone of character."

III MY VOICE IS BECOME WEAK

I am now an obscure member of a nation, that formerly honored and respected my opinions. The path to glory is rough and many gloomy hours obscure it. May the Great Spirit shed light on yours — and that you may never experience the humility that the power of the American government has reduced me to, is the wish of him, who, in his native forests, was once as proud and bold as yourself.

Ma-ke-tai-me-she-kia-kiak, or
Black Hawk, to General H.
Atkinson, 1833

Cowichan Tule Gatherer

Yes — we know that when you come, *we die.*

Chiparopai, an old
Yuma Indian

The war dance was usually performed in the evening. It was only brought out on prominent occasions, or at domestic councils of unusual interest. In the dance, the war-whoop and the response always preceded each song. It was given by the leader, and answered by the band. Anyone present was at liberty to make a speech at any stage of the dance. The speeches were often pleasantries between individuals or strictures upon each other's foibles or perhaps reminders of patriotic feeling. The following is a speech spoken by O-no'-sa.

FRIENDS AND RELATIVES, WE HAVE REASON TO GLORY IN THE achievements of our ancestors. I behold with sadness the present declining state of our noble race. Once the warlike yell and the painted band were the terror of the white man. Then our fathers were strong, and their power was felt and acknowledged far and wide over the American continent. But we have been reduced and broken by the cunning and rapacity of the white-skinned race. We are now compelled to crave, as a blessing, that we may be allowed to live upon our own lands, to cultivate our own fields, to drink from our own springs, and to mingle our bones with those of our fathers. Many winters ago, our wise ancestors predicted that a great monster, with white eyes, would come from the east, and, as he advanced, would consume the land. This monster is the white race. and the prediction is near its fulfillment. They advised their children, when they became weak, to plant a tree with four roots, branching to the north, the south, the east, and the west; and then collecting under its shade, to dwell together in unity and harmony. This tree, I propose, shall be this very spot. Here we will gather, here live, and here die.

Shabonee (or Shabbona), a peace chief and spokesman of the Potawatomi, was born on the Maumee River in Ohio, in 1775, and died in 1859. Many times he saved the white settlements from destruction by warning them of intended Indian uprisings. In 1832, the leader of one such uprising, Black Hawk, asked him twice to join his cause, but Shabonee refused. Instead, he tried to persuade Black Hawk to give up his plans, and when this failed, he warned the nearby settlers. In revenge, the Sauk and Foxes killed Shabonee's son and nephew.

Earlier, during the Winnebago War with the settlers in 1827, Shabonee had also refused to contribute his aid, giving his reasons to two Winnebago chiefs.

IN MY YOUTHFUL DAYS, I HAVE SEEN LARGE HERDS OF BUFFALO on these prairies, and elk were found in every grove, but they are here no more, having gone towards the setting sun. For hundreds of miles no white man lived, but now trading posts and settlers are found here and there throughout the country, and in a few years the smoke from their cabins will be seen to ascend from every grove, and the prairie covered with their cornfields. . . .

The red man must leave the land of his youth and find a new home in the far west. The armies of the whites are without number, like the sands of the sea, and ruin will follow all tribes that go to war with them.

The signing of the Greenville Treaty at Fort Greenville, Ohio, in August 1795, by Blue Jacket, an influential Shawnee chief, gave to the whites a large area of Indian territory. Tecumseh, also a Shawnee chief, dismissed the treaty as worthless and an outright fraud.

MY HEART IS A STONE: HEAVY WITH SADNESS FOR MY PEOPLE; COLD with the knowledge that no treaty will keep whites out of our lands; hard with the determination to resist as long as I live and breathe. Now we are weak and many of our people are afraid. But hear me: a single twig breaks, but the bundle of twigs is strong. Someday I will embrace our brother tribes and draw them into a bundle and together we will win our country back from the whites.

"I am an orator; I was born an orator," the Seneca chief Red Jacket often boasted, and showed (in the words of a biographer) a "remarkable gift for defensive debate." He was a great defender of his people's way of life and continually tried to prevent the sale of their land. In his own life he was often accused of cowardice and treachery, but his skills in verbal eloquence always tended to override these charges. In the spring of 1792, in Philadelphia, the Seneca chief received a silver medal from President George Washington, as a token of friendship and esteem. From that day on, he wore the medal proudly, and since that time, similar medals given to other Indians became known as "Red Jacket medals."

WE FIRST KNEW YOU A FEEBLE PLANT WHICH WANTED A LITTLE earth whereon to grow. We gave it to you; and afterward, when we could have trod you under our feet, we watered and protected you; and now you have grown to be a mighty tree, whose top reaches the clouds, and whose branches overspread the whole land, whilst we, who were the tall pine of the forest, have become a feeble plant and need your protection.

When you first came here, you clung around our knee and called us *father;* we took you by the hand and called you brothers. You have grown greater than we, so that we can no longer reach up to your hand; but we wish to cling around your knee and be called your children.

Navajo

In 1877, the United States government ordered all Nez Perces out of the Wallowa Valley in Oregon onto the Lapwai Reservation in Idaho. The order was in complete violation of the agreement of 1873 which restricted the Wallowa Valley from white settlement. Chief Joseph and his band of Nez Perces were given thirty days to remove themselves and all their possessions by General Oliver Howard. Joseph thought this to be impossible, and asked for more time. "If you let the time run over one day," replied Howard, "the soldiers will be there to drive you onto the reservation, and all your cattle and horses outside of the reservation at that time will fall into the hands of the white men." A council was held and they decided to move immediately.

THE WHITE MEN WERE MANY AND WE COULD NOT HOLD OUR OWN with them. We were like deer. They were like grizzly bears. We had a small country. Their country was large. We were contented to let things remain as the Great Spirit made them. They were not, and would change the rivers if they did not suit them.

Upon General Howard's order, in 1877, Chief Joseph and his small band of Nez Perces vacated their ancient home of the Wallowa Valley and began their journey to the Lapwai Reservation. Before reaching their destination, however, collisions with white settlers took place, causing the Nez Perces to go on the warpath where the whites were severely beaten. Pursued by General Nelson Miles of the United States forces, Chief Joseph was cut off and forced to surrender on October 5, 1877. He and his band were removed to Fort Leavenworth, Kansas, and then to Indian territory.

Chief Joseph's surrender speech is perhaps the most famous and most admired of all such speeches. Oratory was a highly developed art among the Nez Perces, says Herbert J. Spinden, "for on this depended much of the power and prestige of the chiefs. The rule of the council was unanimity, and this would be effected only by calm reasoning where facts were to be considered, and by impassioned appeal when the decision depended on sentiment. . . . Statements were concise and concrete."

TELL GENERAL HOWARD I KNOW HIS HEART. WHAT HE TOLD ME before I have in my heart. I am tired of fighting. Our chiefs are killed. Looking Glass is dead. It is the young men who say yes or no. He who led the young men is dead. It is cold and we have no blankets. The little children are freezing to death. My people, some of them have run away to the hills and have no blankets, no food; no one knows where they are — perhaps freezing to death. I want to have time to look for my children and see how many I can find. Maybe I shall find them among the dead. Hear me my chiefs. I am tired; my heart is sick and sad. From where the sun now stands, I will fight no more forever.

Ollokot was Chief Joseph's brother; he was killed along with many others in the Nez Perce battle of September 1877. Ollokot's surviving widow, Wetatonmi, spoke the following words upon the occasion of leaving the tribe's land the night of Chief Joseph's surrender, just after Joseph had been defeated in battle.

IT WAS LONESOME, THE LEAVING. HUSBAND DEAD, FRIENDS BURIED or held prisoners. I felt that I was leaving all that I had but I did not cry. You know how you feel when you lose kindred and friends through sickness — death. You do not care if you die. With us it was worse. Strong men, well women and little children killed and buried. They had not done wrong to be so killed. We had only asked to be left in our own homes, the homes of our ancestors. Our going was with heavy hearts, broken spirits. But we would be free.... All lost, we walked silently on into the wintry night.

Chief Joseph, Nez Perce

On January 14, 1879, Chief Joseph addressed a large gathering of cabinet members and congressmen. He appealed to President Hayes to allow what was left of his tribe, whose members were dying by the score, to return to their old territory in the Northwest. His appeal was ultimately successful and in 1883, a small party of women and children were allowed to go back to their old home. Joseph was never granted this privilege and spent his remaining days on the Colville Reservation at Nespelim, Washington. He died there September 21, 1904.

I HAVE SHAKEN HANDS WITH A GREAT MANY FRIENDS, BUT THERE are some things I want to know which no one seems able to explain. I cannot understand how the Government hands a man out to fight us, as it did General Miles, and then breaks his word. Such a Government has something wrong about it. . . . I do not understand why nothing is done for my people. I have heard talk and talk, but nothing is done. Good words do not last long until they amount to something. Words do not pay for my dead people. They do not pay for my country, now overrun by white men. They do not protect my father's grave. They do not pay for my horses and cattle.

Good words do not give me back my children. Good words will not make good the promise of your war chief, General Miles. Good words will not give my people good health and stop them from dying. Good words will not get my people a home where they can live in peace and take care of themselves.

I am tired of talk that comes to nothing. It makes my heart sick when I remember all the good words and all the broken promises. There has been too much talking by men who had no right to talk. Too many misinterpretations have been made; too many misunderstandings have come up between the white men about the Indians.

If the white man wants to live in peace with the Indian he can live in peace. There need be no trouble. Treat all men alike. Give them all the same law. Give them all an even chance to live and grow. . . . You might as well expect the rivers to run backward as that any man who was born free should be contented penned up and denied liberty to go where he pleases. If you tie a horse to a stake, do you expect he will grow fat? If you pen an Indian up on a small spot of earth and compel him to stay there, he will not be contented nor will he grow and prosper.

I have asked some of the Great White Chiefs where they get their authority to say to the Indian that he will stay in one place, while he sees white men going where they please. They cannot tell me.

I only ask of the government to be treated as all other men are treated. If I cannot go to my own home, let me have a home in a country where my people will not die so fast. . . .

I know that my race must change. We cannot hold our own with the white men as we are. We only ask an even chance to live as other men live. We ask to be recognized as men. We ask that the same law shall work alike on all men. If an Indian breaks the law, punish him by the law. If a white man breaks the law, punish him also.

Let me be a free man — free to travel, free to stop, free to work, free to trade where I choose, free to choose my own teachers, free to follow the religion of my fathers, free to think and talk and act for myself — and I will obey every law or submit to the penalty.

Chiparopai, an old Yuma Indian, gives her views of the changes that confronted her at the beginning of the twentieth century.

SICKNESS COMES WITH YOU [THE WHITE MAN] AND HUNDREDS OF US die. Where is our strength? . . . In the old times we were strong. We used to hunt and fish. We raised our little crop of corn and melons and ate the mesquite beans. Now all is changed. We eat the white man's food, and it makes us soft; we wear the white man's heavy clothing and it makes us weak. Each day in the old times in summer and in winter we came down to the river banks to bathe. This strengthened and toughened our firm skin. But white settlers were shocked to see the naked Indians, so now we keep away. In old days we wore the breechcloth, and aprons made of bark and reeds. We worked all winter in the wind — bare arms, bare legs, and never felt the cold. But now, when the wind blows down from the mountains it makes us cough. Yes — we know that when you come, *we die.*

Winter, Apsaroke

Apache

Opposed to immigration and hoping that his tribe, the Choctaws, could stay for a while longer in their homes east of the Mississippi, a leading chief of the tribe, Colonel Cobb, addresses a government agent who has come to remove them.

BROTHER! WE HAVE LISTENED TO YOUR TALK, COMING FROM OUR Father, the Great White Chief, at Washington, and my people have called upon me to reply to you. . . .

Brother! we have, as your friends, fought by your side, and have poured out our blood in your defense, but our arms are now broken. You have grown large. My people have become small, and there are none who take pity on them.

Brother! my voice is become weak — you can scarcely hear me. It is not the shout of a warrior, but the wail of an infant. I have lost it in mourning over the desolation and injuries of my people. These are their graves which you see scattered around us, and in the winds which pass through these aged pines we hear the moanings of their departed Ghosts. Their ashes lie here, and we have been left to protect them. Our warriors are nearly all gone to the West, but here are our dead. Will you compel us to go too, and give their bones to the wolves?

Brother! our heart is full. Twelve winters ago we were told our Chiefs had sold our country. Every warrior that you now see around us was opposed to the Treaty; and if the voice of our people could have been heard, that act would never have been done; but alas! though they stood around they could neither be seen nor heard. Their tears fell like drops of rain — their lamentations were borne away by the passing winds — the pale-faces heeded them not and our land was taken from us.

Brother! . . . you speak the words of a mighty nation. I am a shadow, and scarcely reach to your knee. My people are scattered and gone; when I shout, I hear my voice in the depths of the forest, but no answering voice comes back to me — all is silent around me! My words therefore must be few. I can now say no more.

Blanket Weaver, Navajo

Keokuk, a Sauk leader, was born about 1780 on the banks of the Rock River, Illinois, and died in 1848. After the Black Hawk Purchase in 1832, the Indians were obliged to leave their land. In his farewell, Keokuk voices an unusual generosity.

BROTHER! MY PEOPLE AND MYSELF HAVE COME TO SHAKE HANDS with you. The time for us to go hàs come. We do not feel glad to leave this country which we have lived in so long.

The many moons and sunny days we have lived here will long be remembered by us. The Great Spirit has smiled upon us and made us glad. But we have agreed to go.

We go to a country we know but little of. Our new home will be beyond a great river on the way to the setting sun. We will build our wigwams there in another land where we hope the Great Spirit will smile upon us; as he has here.

The men we leave here in possession of these lands cannot say Keokuk and his people have ever taken up the tomahawk . . . against them. We have always been for peace with you, and you have been kind to us. In peace we bid you good-bye. May the Great Spirit smile upon you in this land, and upon us in the new land to which we go. We will think of you and you must think of us. If you come to see us, we will divide our supply of venison with you and we will gladly welcome.

In an address to General George Washington in 1791 at Philadelphia (then the seat of government), Seneca Chief Cornplant pleads with the President to restore to his nation the land which was taken from them in the Treaty of Fort Stanwix a few years earlier.

FATHER! THE VOICE OF THE SENECA NATION SPEAKS TO YOU, THE Great Counsellor, in whose heart the wise men of all the thirteen fires [thirteen states], have placed their wisdom. What we may have to say may appear small in your ears and we therefore entreat you to hearken with attention, for we are about to speak of things of very great importance.

When your army entered the country of the Six Nations we called you the TOWN DESTROYER, and to this day, when that terrible name is heard, our women look behind and turn pale, and our children cling to the breasts of their mothers. Our Counsellors and Warriors are men, and cannot be afraid, but their hearts are grieved on account of the distress of our women and children.

[Cornplant then set forth in detail the stratagems and other iniquitous means that had been used to deceive the Indians, compelling them to surrender the great country lately given up. He referred to the part he had himself been led to take in making the treaty, describing the effect produced on the minds of his people towards him.]

Father! When that great country was surrendered, there were but few Chiefs present, and they were compelled to give it up and it is not the Six Nations only that reproach these Chiefs with having giving up that country; the Chippewas, and all the Nations who lived on those Lands, westward, call to us and ask us, "brothers of our fathers, where is the place you have reserved for us to lie down upon?"

Father! you have compelled us to do that which has made us ashamed. We have nothing to answer to the children of the brothers of our fathers. When, last Spring, they called upon us to go to war, to secure a bed to lie upon, the Senecas entreated them to be quiet, until we had spoken to you. . . .

Father! we will not conceal from you, that the Great God, and not man, has preserved Cornplant from the hands of his own Nation; for they ask continually: "where is the Land which our children, and their children after them are to lie upon?" You told us, they say, "that the line drawn from Pennsylvania to Lake

Flathead Chief

Ontario, would mark it forever on the East; and the line running from Beaver Creek to Pennsylvania, would mark it on the West, and we see that it is not so. For first one, and then another, comes and takes it away, by order of that people which *you* tell us promised to secure it to us." He is silent, for he has nothing to answer. When the Sun goes down, he opens his heart before his God, and earlier than the Sun appears upon the hills, he gives thanks for his protection during the night; for he feels that among men, made desperate by their wrongs, it is God alone that can preserve him. He loves peace, and all that he had in store he has given to those who have been robbed by your people, lest they should plunder the innocent to repay themselves. The whole season, while others have been employed in providing for their families, he has spent in his endeavors to preserve peace, and at this moment his wife and children are lying on the ground, and in want of food; his heart is pained for them, but he perceives that the Great God will try his firmness in doing what is right.

Father! you have said we are in your hand, and that by shutting it you could crush us to nothing. Are you determined to crush us? . . .

Father! innocent men of our Nation are killed, one after another, and of our best families, but none of your people who have committed these murders have been punished. We now ask you, was it intended that your people should kill the Senecas, and not only remain unpunished by you, but be protected by you against the revenge of the next of kin?

Father! these are to us very great things. We know that you are very strong — we have heard you are wise — and we now wait to receive your answer to what we have said, that we may know if you are just.

numerous versions exist of the fatal stabbing of Crazy Horse at Camp Robinson, which occurred a few months after his surrender to reservation life in 1877. Of his surrender, Chief Luther Standing Bear maintains that Crazy Horse "foresaw the consequence." "It meant submission to a people whom he did not consider his equal; it meant the doom of his race. Crazy Horse feared no man and when he did surrender, it was not from volition on his part but because his people were tired of warfare."

In the version of his death by Major H.R. Lemly, who had been stationed at Camp Robinson, Crazy Horse defended his character as he was dying.

I WAS NOT HOSTILE TO THE WHITE MAN. OCCASIONALLY MY YOUNG men would attack a party of the Crows or Arickarees, and take their ponies, but just as often, they were the assailants. We had buffalo for food, and their hides for clothing, and we preferred the chase to a life of idleness and the bickerings and jealousies, as well as the frequent periods of starvation at the Agencies.

But the Gray Fox [General Crook] came out in the snow and bitter cold, and destroyed my village. All of us would have perished of exposure and hunger had we not recaptured our ponies.

Then Long Hair [Custer] came in the same way. They say we massacred him, but he would have massacred us had we not defended ourselves and fought to the death. Our first impulse was to escape with our squaws and papooses, but we were so hemmed in that we had to fight. . . .

Again the Gray Fox sent soldiers to surround me and my village; but I was tired of fighting. All I wanted was to be let alone, so I anticipated their coming and marched all night to Spotted Tail Agency while the troops were approaching the site of my camp. Touch-the-Clouds knows how I settled at Spotted Tail Agency, in peace. The agent told me I must first talk with the big white chief of the Black Hills. Under his care I came here unarmed, but instead of talking, they tried to confine me, and when I made an effort to escape, a soldier ran his bayonet into me.

I HAVE SPOKEN.

Then, writes Major Lemly, "in a weak and tremulous voice, he broke into the weird and now-famous death song of the Sioux. Instantly there were two answering calls from beyond the line of pickets, and Big Bat told me they were from Crazy Horse's old father and mother, who begged to see their dying son. I had no authority to admit them, and resisted their appeal, piteous as it was, until Crazy Horse fell back with the death-gurgle in his throat."

Koskimo Fire Drill

Chief Plenty-Coups gives a farewell address in 1909 at the Little Bighorn council grounds in Montana.

THE GROUND ON WHICH WE STAND IS SACRED GROUND. IT IS THE dust and blood of our ancestors. On these plains the Great White Father at Washington sent his soldiers armed with long knives and rifles to slay the Indian. Many of them sleep on yonder hill where Pahaska — White Chief of the Long Hair [General Custer] — so bravely fought and fell. A few more passing suns will see us here no more, and our dust and bones will mingle with these same prairies. I see as in a vision the dying spark of our council fires, the ashes cold and white. I see no longer the curling smoke rising from our lodge poles. I hear no longer the songs of the women as they prepare the meal. The antelope have gone; the buffalo wallos are empty. Only the wail of the coyote is heard. The white man's medicine is stronger than ours; his iron horse rushes over the buffalo trail. He talks to us through his 'whispering spirit' [the telephone]. We are like birds with a broken wing. My heart is cold within me. My eyes are growing dim — I am old. . . .

Hesquiat Root Digger

When the Choctaws signed the Treaty at Dancing Rabbit Creek, September 27, 1830, they gave up the last acre of their land in the state of Mississippi. By the new treaty they were required to move to a region west of the Arkansas. The sixteenth article of the treaty provided that the United States government should remove at its own expense the 20,000 members or so of the nation "in wagons, and with steamboats as may be found necessary." George W. Harkins, a district chief of the Choctaw Nation, expressed the feelings of his people as they left the Mississippi on board a steamship, in an address which appeared in the press in the winter of 1832.

TO THE AMERICAN PEOPLE:

It is with considerable difficulty that I attempt to address the American people, knowing and feeling sensibly my incompetency, and believing that your highly and well improved minds could not be well entertained by the address of a Choctaw. But having determined to emigrate west of the Mississippi river this fall, I have thought proper in bidding you farewell to make a few remarks of my views and the feelings that actuate me on the subject of our removal. . . .

We were hedged in by two evils, and we chose that which we thought least. Yet we could not recognize the right that the state of Mississippi had assumed to legislate for us. Although the legislature of the state were qualified to make laws for their own citizens, that did not qualify them to become law makers to a people who were so dissimilar in manners and customs as the Choctaws are to the Mississippians. Admitting that they understood the people, could they remove that mountain of prejudice that has ever obstructed the streams of justice, and prevented their salutary influence from reaching my devoted countrymen? We as Choctaws rather chose to suffer and be free, than live under the degrading influence of laws where our voice could not be heard in their formation.

Much as the state of Mississippi has wronged us, I cannot find in my heart any other sentiment than an ardent wish for her prosperity and happiness.

I could cheerfully hope that those of another age and generation may not feel the effects of those oppressive measures that have been so illiberally dealt out to us; and that peace and happiness may be their reward. Amid the gloom and honors of our present separation, we are cheered with a hope that ere long we shall reach our destined home, and that nothing short of the basest acts of treachery will ever be able to wrest it from us, and that we may live free. Although your ancestors won freedom on the fields of danger and glory, our ancestors owned it as their birthright, and we have had to purchase it from you as the vilest slaves buy their freedom. . . .

But such is the instability of professions. The man who said that he would plant a stake and draw a line around us, that never should be passed, was the first to say that he could not guard the lines, and drew up the stake and wiped out all traces of the line. I will not conceal from you my fears, that the present grounds may be removed. I have my foreboding — who of us can tell after witnessing what has already been done, what the next force may be.

I ask you in the name of justice for repose, for myself and my injured people. Let us alone — we will not harm you, we want rest. We hope, in the name of justice that another outrage may never be committed against us. . . .

Friends, my attachment to my native land is strong — that cord is now broken; and we must go forth as wanderers in a strange land! I must go — let me entreat you to regard us with feelings of kindness, and when the hand of oppression is stretched against us, let me hope that every part of the United States, filling the mountains and valleys, will echo and say stop. . . .

Yours with respect,
George W. Harkins.

Ma-ke-tai-me-she-kia-kiak, or Black Hawk, was chief of the Sauk and Fox Indians and leader in the Black Hawk War of 1832. After the war of 1812, white settlers began to stream into Illinois country, old Sauk and Fox territory. The majority of the Indians, under Keokuk, moved across the Mississippi; but Black Hawk declined to leave and in 1832 as chief of the remaining Sauks and Foxes declared war against the new settlements. He was captured the same year and taken east for imprisonment. The following speech is said to be the speech he made when he surrendered himself at Prairie du Chien, Wisconsin, August 27, 1832.

YOU HAVE TAKEN ME PRISONER WITH ALL MY WARRIORS. I AM MUCH grieved, for I expected, if I did not defeat you, to hold out much longer, and give you more trouble before I surrendered. I tried hard to bring you into ambush, but your last general understands Indian fighting. The first one was not so wise. When I saw I could not beat you by Indian fighting, I determined to rush on you, and fight you face to face. I fought hard. But your guns were well aimed. The bullets flew like birds in the air, and whizzed by our ears like the wind through the trees in the winter. My warriors fell around me; it began to look dismal. I saw my evil day at hand. The sun rose dim on us in the morning, and at night it sunk in a dark cloud, and looked like a ball of fire. That was the last sun that shone on Black Hawk. His heart is dead, and no longer beats quick in his bosom. He is now a prisoner to the white men; they will do with him as they wish. But he can stand torture, and is not afraid of death. He is no coward. Black Hawk is an Indian.

He has done nothing for which an Indian ought to be ashamed. He has fought for his countrymen, the squaws and papooses, against white men, who came year after year, to cheat them and take away their lands. You know the cause of our making war. It is known to all white men. They ought to be ashamed of it. Indians are not deceitful. The white men speak bad of the Indian and look at him spitefully. But the Indian does not tell lies; Indians do not steal.

An Indian who is as bad as the white men could not live in our nation; he would be put to death, and eaten up by the wolves. The white men are bad schoolmasters; they carry false books, and deal in false actions; they smile in the face of the poor Indian to cheat him; they shake them by the hand to gain their confidence, to make them drunk, to deceive them, and ruin our wives. We told them to leave us alone, and keep away from us; but they followed on, and beset our paths, and they coiled themselves among us, like the snake. They poisoned us by their touch. We were not safe. We lived in danger. We were becoming like them, hypocrites and liars, adulterous lazy drones, all talkers, and no workers.

We looked up to the Great Spirit. We went to our great father. We were encouraged. His great council gave us fair words and big promises; but we got no satisfaction. Thing were growing worse. There were no deer in the forest. The opossum and beaver were fled; the springs were drying up; and our squaws and papooses were without victuals to keep them from starving. We called a great council, and built a large fire. The spirit of our fathers arose and spoke to us to avenge our wrongs or die. We all spoke before the council fire. It was warm and pleasant. We set up the war-whoop, and dug up the tomahawk; our knives were ready, and the heart of Black Hawk swelled high in the bosom, when he led his warriors to battle. He is satisfied. He will go to the world of spirits contented. He has done his duty. His father will meet him there and commend him.

Black Hawk is a true Indian, and disdains to cry like a woman. He feels for his wife, his children and friends. But he does not care for himself. He cares for his nation and the Indians. They will suffer. He laments their fate. The white men do not scalp the head; but they do worse — they poison the heart. It is not pure with them. His countrymen will not be scalped, but they will, in a few years, become like the white men, so that you can't trust them, and there must be, as in the white settlements, nearly as many officers as men to take care of them and keep them in order.

Farewell, my nation! Black Hawk tried to save you, and avenge your wrongs. He drank the blood of some of the whites. He has been taken prisoner, and his plans are stopped. He can do no more. He is near his end. His sun is setting, and he will rise no more. Farewell to Black Hawk.

Kutenai Duck Hunter

In 1833, Black Hawk dictated his autobiography to Antoine LeClair. In it appears his dedication to Brigadier General H. Atkinson, the "White Beaver" — "the great war chief who commanded the American army against my little band" leading to Black Hawk's surrender.

SIR, — THE CHANGES OF FORTUNE, AND VICISSITUDES OF WAR, MADE you my conqueror. When my last resources were exhausted, my warriors worn down with long and toilsome marches, we yielded, and I became your prisoner.

The story of my life is told in the following pages; it is intimately connected, and in some measure, identified with a part of the history of your own: I have, therefore, dedicated it to you.

The changes of many summers have brought old age upon me, — and I cannot expect to survive many moons. Before I set out on my journey to the land of my fathers, I have determined to give my motives and reasons for my former hostilities to the whites, and to vindicate my character from misrepresentation. The kindness I received from you whilst a prisoner of war, assures me that you will vouch for the facts contained in my narrative, so far as they came under your observation.

I am now an obscure member of a nation, that formerly honored and respected my opinions. The path to glory is rough, and many gloomy hours obscure it. May the Great Spirit shed light on yours — and that you may never experience the humility that the power of the American government has reduced me to, is the wish of him, who, in his native forests, was once as proud and bold as yourself.

Black Hawk

10th Moon, 1833.

Sitting Bull had surrendered at Fort Buford, Canada, in 1881, "under promise of amnesty," and was later sent to the Standing Rock Agency where most of his people lived. When the United States delegation arrived asking him to return to the United States, he began his response by handing his rifle to his eight-year-old son, instructing him to give it to Major Brotherton of the Northwest Mounted Police.

I SURRENDER THIS RIFLE TO YOU THROUGH MY SON. I WISH HIM TO learn the habits of whites. I wish it to be remembered that I was the last man of my tribe to surrender my rifle, and this day have given it to you. Whatever you have to give, or whatever you have to say, I would like to receive of here now, for I don't wish to be kept in darkness longer. I have sent several messengers here from time to time, but none of them have returned with news. The other chiefs, Crow King and Gall, have not wanted me to come and I have never received good news from them. I now wish to be allowed to live this side of the line [Canada] or the other, as I see fit. I wish to continue my old life of hunting, but would like to be allowed to trade on both sides of the line. This [Canada] is my country, and I don't wish to be compelled to give it up. My heart was very sad at having to leave the Great Mother's country. She has been a friend to me, but I want my children to grow up in our native country. . . . I wish to have all my people live together upon one reservation of our own on the Little Missouri. I left several families at Wood Mountain, and between there and Qu'Appelle. I have many people among the Yanktons at Poplar Creek, and I wish all of them and those who have gone to Standing Rock to be collected together upon my reservation.

Confined to the Cheyenne-Arapahoe Reservation near Fort Reno in August 1877, the northern Cheyennes were plagued by sickness and death. After a year in such circumstances, two chiefs, Dull Knife and Little Wolf, went to plead with Indian agent John D. Miles to allow the Indians to go back to their home in the Black Hills country. Dull Knife, in fact, was too ill to talk, and Little Wolf had to speak for both.

WE HAVE COME TO ASK THE AGENT THAT WE BE SENT HOME TO OUR own country in the mountains. My people were raised there, in a land of pines and clear, cold rivers. There, we were always healthy, for there was meat enough for all. We were happy there until the Great Father's soldiers brought us here. Now, in the year that we have been in this southern country, many of us have died. This is not a good place for us — there is too much heat and dust and not enough food. We wish to return to our home in the mountains. If you have not the power to give us permission to go back there, let some of us go on to Washington and tell them there how it is; or do you write to Washington and get permission for us to go back North? . . . We cannot stay another year; we want to go now. Before another year has passed, we may all be dead, and there will be none of us left to travel north.

Trout Trap, Hupa

In the Moon of the Changing Season, October 16, 1867, one of the most notable Indian councils in the history of the country began at Medicine Lodge, Kansas. The Medicine Lodge peace council brought together well over 4,000 Indians, including the Arapahos, Cheyennes, Kiowas, Comanches and Prairie Apaches. A new peace plan by the government sought to establish all five tribes on one great reservation south of the Arkansas River. A memorable speech was made by Parra-Wa-Samen, Ten Bears, more a poet than a Comanche warrior chief, who signed the treaty along with the others. He died five years later.

MY HEART IS FILLED WITH JOY WHEN I SEE YOU HERE, AS THE brooks fill with water when the snow melts in the spring; and I feel glad as the ponies do when the fresh grass starts in the beginning of the year. . . .

My people have never first drawn a bow or fired a gun against the whites. There has been trouble on the line between us, and my young men have danced the war dance. But it was not begun by us. It was you who sent the first soldier and we who sent out the second. Two years ago I came upon this road, following the buffalo, that my wives and children might have their cheeks plump and their bodies warm. But the soldiers fired on us, and since that time, there has been a noise like that of a thunderstorm, and we have not known which way to go. . . .

Nor have we been made to cry once alone. The blue dressed soldiers and the Utes came from out of the night when it was dark and still, and for campfires they lit our lodges. Instead of hunting game they killed my braves, and the warriors of the tribe cut their hair for the dead. So it was in Texas. They made sorrow come into our camps, and we went out like the buffalo bulls when their cows are attacked. When we found them, we killed them and their scalps hang in our lodges.

The Comanches are not weak and blind, like the pups of the dog when seven sleeps old. They are strong and far-sighted, like grown horses. We took their road and we went on it. The white women cried and our women laughed.

But there are things which you have said to me which I do not like. They were not sweet like sugar, but bitter like gourds. You said that you wanted to put us upon a reservation, to build us houses and make us medicine lodges. I do not want them. I was born upon the prairie where the wind blew free and there was nothing to break the light of the sun. I was born where there were no enclosures and where everything drew a free breath. I want to die there and not within walls. I know every stream and every wood between the Rio Grande and the Arkansas; I have hunted and lived over that country. I lived like my fathers before me, and, like them, I lived happily.

When I was at Washington, the Great Father told me that all the Comanche land was ours and that no one should hinder us in living upon it. So why do you ask us to leave the rivers and the sun and the wind and live in houses? Do not ask us to give up the buffalo for the sheep. The young men have heard talk of this, and it has made them sad and angry. . . .

If the Texans had kept out of my country there might have been peace. But that which you now say we must live on is too small. The Texans have taken away the places where the grass grew the thickest and the timber was the best. Had we kept that, we might have done the things you ask. But it is too late. The white man has the country which we loved, and we only wish to wander on the prairies until we die.

Geronimo, Apache

Goyathlay, or Geronimo, told the story of his life, in 1905, to Asa Daklugie, the son of a hostile Apache chief who fought with Geronimo in the last campaigns. Daklugie then translated the story for S.M. Barrett, who was superintendent of education in nearby Lawton, Oklahoma.

In August 1877, Geronimo and his band had surrendered for the last time; the entire band (about 340) had been deported as prisoners of war, and finally they settled on a reservation at Fort Sill, Oklahoma. It is from here that Geronimo made his plea to the President to be allowed to return to his homeland before he dies.

THERE IS A GREAT QUESTION BETWEEN THE APACHES AND THE Government. For twenty years we have been held prisoners of war under a treaty which was made with General Miles, on the part of the United States Government, and myself as the representative of the Apaches. That treaty has not at all times been properly observed by the Government, although at the present time it is being more nearly fulfilled on their part than heretofore. In the treaty with General Miles we agreed to go to a place outside of Arizona and learn to live as the white people do. I think that my people are now capable of living in accordance with the laws of the United States, and we would, of course, like to have the liberty to return to that land which is ours by divine right. We are reduced in numbers, and having learned how to cultivate the soil would not require so much ground as was formerly necessary. We do not ask all of the land which the Almighty gave us in the beginning, but that we may have sufficient lands there to cultivate. What we do not need we are glad for the white men to cultivate.

We are now held on Comanche and Kiowa lands, which are not suited to our needs. . . . Our people are decreasing in numbers here, and will continue to decrease unless they are allowed to return to their native land. . . .

There is no climate or soil which, to my mind, is equal to that of Arizona. We could have plenty of good cultivating land, plenty of grass, plenty of timber and plenty of minerals in that land which the Almighty created for the Apaches. It is my land, my home, my fathers' land, to which I now ask to be allowed to return. I want to spend my last days there, and be buried among those mountains. If this could be I might die in peace, feeling that my people, placed in their native homes, would increase in numbers, rather than diminish as at present, and that our name would not become extinct.

I know that if my people were placed in that mountainous region lying around the headwaters of the Gila River [in New Mexico] they would live in peace and act according to the will of the President. They would be prosperous and happy in tilling the soil and learning the civilization of the white men, whom they now respect. Could I but see this accomplished, I think I could forget all the wrongs that I have ever received, and die a contented and happy old man. But we can do nothing in this matter ourselves — we must wait until those in authority choose to act. If this cannot be done during my lifetime — if I must die in bondage — I hope that the remnant of the Apache tribe may, when I am gone, be granted the one privilege which they request — to return to Arizona.

Hehaka Sapa, or Black Elk, the holy man of the Sioux, tells of the spiritual improverishment suffered by his people when they were obliged to leave their old homeland and take up the white man's ways.

THE WASICHUS HAVE PUT US IN THESE SQUARE BOXES. OUR POWER IS gone and we are dying, for the power is not in us any more. You can look at our boys and see how it is with us. When we were living by the power of the circle in the way we should, boys were men at twelve or thirteen. But now it takes them very much longer to mature. Well, it is as it is. We are prisoners of war while we are waiting here. But there is another world.

Apsaroke

In his autobiography, Geronimo discusses the importance of the fit between a land and its people, and its effect upon the spirit and life of the Apache people.

WE ARE VANISHING FROM THE EARTH, YET I CANNOT THINK WE ARE useless or Usen [Apache word for God] would not have created us. . . .

For each tribe of men Usen created, He also made a home. In the land created for any particular tribe He placed whatever would be best for the welfare of that tribe.

When Usen created the Apaches He also created their homes in the West. He gave them such grain, fruits, and game as they needed to eat. To restore their health when disease attacked them He taught them where to find these herbs, and how to prepare them for medicine. He gave them a pleasant climate and all they needed for clothing and shelter was at hand.

Thus it was in the beginning: the Apaches and their homes each created for the other by Usen himself. When they are taken from these homes they sicken and die. How long will it be until it is said there are no Apaches?

This prayer by Black Elk was delivered from Harney Peak in the Black Hills, in 1931.

HEY-A-A-HEY! HEY-A-A-HEY! HEY-A-A-HEY! GRANDFATHER, GREAT Spirit, once more behold me on earth and lean to hear my feeble voice. You lived first, and you are older than all need, older than all prayer. All things belong to you — the two-leggeds, the four-leggeds, the wings of the air and all green things that live. You have set the powers of the four quarters to cross each other. The good road and the road of difficulties you have made to cross; and where they cross, the place is holy. Day in and day out, forever, you are the life of things....

You have said to me, when I was still young and could hope, that in difficulty I should send a voice four times, once for each quarter of the earth....

Today I send a voice for a people in despair.

From the west, you have given me the cup of living water and the sacred bow, the power to make live and to destroy. You have given me a sacred wind and the herb from where the white giant lives — the cleansing power and the healing. The daybreak star and the pipe, you have given from the east; and from the south, the nations' sacred hoop and the tree that was to bloom. To the center of the world you have taken me and showed the goodness and beauty and the strangeness of the greening earth, the only mother — and there the spirit shapes of things, as they should be, you have shown to me and I have seen. At the center of this sacred hoop you have said that I should make the tree to bloom.

With tears running, O Great Spirit, Great Spirit, my Grandfather — with running tears I must say that the tree has never bloomed. A pitiful old man, you see me here, and I have fallen away and have done nothing. Here at the center of the world, where you took me when I was young and taught; here, old, I stand, and the tree is withered, Grandfather, my Grandfather!

Again, and maybe the last time on this earth, I recall the great vision you sent me. It may be that some little root of the sacred tree still lives. Nourish it then, that it may leaf and bloom and fill with singing birds. Hear me, not for myself, but for my people; I am old. Hear me that they may once more go back into the sacred hoop and find the good red road, the shielding tree!

In sorrow I am sending a feeble voice, O Six Powers of the World. Hear me in my sorrow, for I may never call again. O make my people live!

Khe-tha-a-hi, or Eagle Wing, pays tribute to what the Indian has left behind him.

MY BROTHERS, THE INDIANS MUST ALWAYS BE REMEMBERED IN THIS land. Out of our languages we have given names to many beautiful things which will always speak of us. Minnehaha will laugh of us, Seneca will shine in our image, Mississippi will murmur our woes. The broad Iowa and the rolling Dakota and the fertile Michigan will whisper our names to the sun that kisses them. The roaring Niagra, the sighing Illinois, the singing Delaware, will chant unceasingly our Dta-wa-e [Death Song]. Can it be that you and your children will hear that eternal song without a stricken heart? We have been guilty of only one sin — we have had possessions that the white man coveted. We moved away toward the setting sun; we gave up our homes to the white man.

My brethren, among the legends of my people it is told how a chief, leading the remnant of his people, crossed a great river, and striking his tipi-stake upon the ground, exclaimed, "A-la-ba-ma!" This in our language means "Here we may rest!" But he saw not the future. The white man came: he and his people could not rest there; they were driven out, and in a dark swamp they were thrust down into the slime and killed. The word he so sadly spoke has given a name to one of the white man's states. There is no spot under those stars that now smile upon us, where the Indian can plant his foot and sigh "A-la-ba-ma." It may be that Wakanda will grant us such a place. But it seems that it will be only at His side.

Where today is the Pequot? Where are the Narragansetts, the Mohawks, the Pokanoket, and many other once powerful tribes of our people? They have vanished before the avarice and the oppression of the White Man, as snow before a summer sun.

Tecumseh, Shawnee Chief

Navajo

IV IF WE SURRENDER, WE DIE

Our ideas will overcome your ideas. We are going to cut the country's whole value system to shreds. It isn't important that there are only 500,000 of us Indians. . . . What is important is that we have a superior way of life. We Indians have a more human philosophy of life. We Indians will show this country how to act human. Someday this country will revise its constitution, its laws, in terms of human beings, instead of property. If Red Power is to be a power in this country it is because it is ideological. . . . What is the ultimate value of a man's life? That is the question.

Vine Deloria, Jr., 1971

Nootka Man

Chief Dan George, a hereditary Chief of the Coast Salish tribe, and honorary Chief of the Squamish tribe in British Columbia, gave a speech in 1967 in Vancouver on the occasion of Canada's one hundredth birthday.

HOW LONG HAVE I KNOWN YOU, OH CANADA? A HUNDRED YEARS? YES, a hundred years. And many many 'seelanum' more. And today, when you celebrate your hundred years, oh Canada, I am sad for all the Indian people throughout the land.

For I have known you when your forests were mine; when they gave me my meat and my clothing. I have known you in your streams and rivers where your fish flashed and danced in the sun, where the waters said come, come and eat of my abundance. I have known you in the freedom of your winds. And my spirit, like the winds, once roamed your good lands.

But in the long hundred years since the white man came, I have seen my freedom disappear like the salmon going mysteriously out to sea. The white man's strange customs which I could not understand, pressed down upon me until I could no longer breathe.

When I fought to protect my land and my home, I was called a savage. When I neither understood nor welcomed this way of life, I was called lazy. When I tried to rule my people, I was stripped of my authority.

My nation was ignored in your history textbooks — they were little more important in the history of Canada than the buffalo that ranged the plains. I was ridiculed in your plays and motion pictures, when I drank your fire-water, I got drunk — very, very drunk. And I forgot.

Oh Canada, how can I celebrate with you this Centenary, this hundred years? Shall I thank you for the reserves that are left to me of my beautiful forests? For the canned fish of my rivers? For the loss of my pride and authority, even among my own people? For the lack of my will to fight back? No! I must forget what's past and gone.

Oh, God in Heaven! Give me back the courage of the olden Chiefs. Let me wrestle with my surroundings. Let me again, as in the days of old, dominate my environment. Let me humbly accept this new culture and through it rise up and go on.

Oh, God! Like the Thunderbird of old I shall rise again out of the sea; I shall grab the instruments of the white man's success — his education, his skills, and with these new tools I shall build my race into the proudest segment of your society. Before I follow the great Chiefs who have gone before us, oh Canada, I shall see these things come to pass.

I shall see our young braves and our chiefs sitting in the houses of law and government, ruling and being ruled by the knowledge and freedom of our great land. So shall we shatter the barriers of our isolation. So shall the next hundred years be the greatest in the proud history of our tribes and nations.

Makah Halibut Fishermen

In November of 1969, a group of Indians seized the island of Alcatraz, the old prison site, which was occupied only by some caretakers. The Indians refused the orders of government officials to leave and were forcibly evicted in June 1971. The following statement explains their claim to the island.

PROCLAMATION: TO THE GREAT WHITE FATHER AND ALL HIS PEOPLE

We, the native Americans, re-claim the land known as Alcatraz Island in the name of all American Indians by right of discovery.

We wish to be fair and honorable in our dealings with the Caucasian inhabitants of this land, and hereby offer the following treaty:

We will purchase said Alcatraz Island for twenty-four dollars ($24) in glass beads and red cloth, a precedent set by the white man's purchase of a similar island about 300 years ago. We know that $24 in trade goods for these 16 acres is more than was paid when Manhattan Island was sold, but we know that land values have risen over the years. Our offer of $1.24 per acre is greater than the 47¢ per acre that the white men are now paying the California Indians for their land. We will give to the inhabitants of this island a portion of that land for their own, to be held in trust by the American Indian Affairs and by the bureau of Caucasian Affairs to hold in perpetuity — for as long as the sun shall rise and the rivers go down to the sea. We will further guide the inhabitants in the proper way of living. We will offer them our religion, our education, our life-ways, in order to help them achieve our level of civilization and thus raise them and all their white brothers up from their savage and unhappy state. We offer this treaty in good faith and wish to be fair and honorable in our dealings with all white men. . . .

We feel that this so-called Alcatraz Island is more than suitable for an Indian Reservation, as determined by the white man's own standards. By this we mean that this place resembles most Indian reservations in that:

1. It is isolated from modern facilities, and without adequate means of transportation.
2. It has no fresh running water.
3. It has inadequate sanitation facilities.
4. There are no oil or mineral rights.
5. There is no industry and so unemployment is very great.
6. There are no health care facilities.

7. The soil is rocky and non-productive; and the land does not support game.
8. There are no educational facilities.
9. The population has always exceeded the land base.
10. The population has always been held as prisoners and kept dependent upon others.

Further, it would be fitting and symbolic that ships from all over the world, entering the Golden Gate, would first see Indian land, and thus be reminded of the true history of this nation. This tiny island would be a symbol of the great lands once ruled by free and noble Indians.

Skokomish Woman

The Wedding Party, Qágyuhî

Harold Cardinal, a Cree Indian, was born in 1945 in High Prairie, Alberta, and raised on the Sucker Creek Cree Reserve. In the last several years he has become a skillful politician, speaking out on behalf of Indian rights in Canada, the history of which rights he describes as "a shameful chronicle of the white man's disinterest . . . [of] his deliberate trampling . . . and [of] his repeated betrayal of our trust." The following passage is taken from his recent book *The Unjust Society, The Tragedy of Canada's Indians.*

OUR PEOPLE NO LONGER BELIEVE. IT IS THAT SIMPLE AND IT IS THAT sad. The Canadian government can promise involvement, consultation, progressive human and economic development programs. We will no longer believe them. . . .

After generations of endless frustration with the Canadian government, our people are tired and impatient. *Before* the Canadian government tries to feed us hypocritical policy statements, more empty promises, more forked tonguistics, our people want, our people, the Indians, demand just settlement of all our treaty and aboriginal rights. Fulfillment of Indian rights by the queen's government must come before there can be any further co-operation between the Indians and the government. We demand nothing more. We expect nothing less.

Yes, the prime minister roused our hopes with his talk of a compassionate and just society. Then his minister for Indian Affairs told us our problems would vanish if we would become nice, manageable white men like all other Canadians. Just recently, the prime minister himself flicked the other fork of his tongue. In a speech in Vancouver, Mr. Trudeau said, "The federal government is not prepared to guarantee the aboriginal rights of Canada's Indians. . . ."

To the Indians of Canada, the treaties represent an Indian Magna Carta. The treaties are important to us, because we entered into these negotiations with faith, with hope for a better life with honor. We have survived for over a century on little but that hope. Did the white man enter into them with something less in mind? Or have the heirs of the men who signed in honor somehow disavowed the obligation passed down to them? The Indians entered into the treaty negotiations as honorable men who came to deal as equals with the queen's representatives. Our leaders of that time thought they were dealing with an equally honorable people. Our leaders pledged themselves, their people and their heirs, to honor what was done then.

Our leaders mistakenly thought they were dealing with an honorable people who would do no less than the Indians were doing — bind themselves, bind their people and bind their heirs to honorable contracts. . . .

The treaties were the way in which the white people legitimized in the eyes of the world their presence in our country. It was an attempt to settle the terms of occupancy on a just basis, legally and morally to extinguish the legitimate claims of our people to title to the land in our country. There never has been any doubt in the minds of our people that the land in Canada belonged to them. . . .

In the language of the Cree Indians, the Indian reserves are known as *the land that we kept for ourselves or the land that we did not give to the government.* In our language, *skun-gun.* . . .

As far as we are concerned our treaty rights represent a sacred, honorable agreement between ourselves and the Canadian government that cannot be unilaterally abrogated by the government at the whim of one of its leaders unless that government is prepared to give us back title to our country.

Our rights are too valuable to surrender to gallic or any other kind of rhetoric, too valuable to be sold for pieces of gold. Words change; the value of money fluctuates, may even disappear; our land will not disappear.

We cannot give up our rights without destroying ourselves as people. If our rights are meaningless, if it is inconceivable that our society have treaties with the white society even though those treaties were signed by honorable men on both sides, in good faith, long before the present government decided to tear them up as worthless scraps of paper, then we as a people are meaningless. We cannot and we will not accept this. We know that as long as we fight for our rights we will survive. If we surrender, we die.

Last year the Peabody Coal Company, a subsidiary of Kennecott Copper Company, began stripping coal from 65,000 acres it has leased from the Navajo and Hopi tribes. Company officials declared that this mining would not damage Indian lands and in fact would improve the lives of many Navajos and Hopis. In disagreement with this action a group of Hopi wrote the following letter to President Nixon:

Dear Mr. President:

WE, THE TRUE AND TRADITIONAL RELIGIOUS LEADERS, RECOGNIZED as such by the Hopi People, maintain full authority over all land and life contained within the Western Hemisphere. We are granted our stewardship by virtue of our instruction as to the meaning of Nature, Peace, and Harmony as spoken to our People by Him, known to us as Massau'u, the Great Spirit, who long ago provided for us the sacred stone tablets which we preserve to this day. For many generations before the coming of the white man, for many generations before the coming of the Navajo, the Hopi People have lived in the sacred place known to you as the Southwest and known to us to be the spiritual center of our continent. Those of us of the Hopi Nation who have followed the path of the Great Spirit without compromise have a message which we are committed, through our prophecy, to convey to you.

The white man, through his insensitivity to the way of Nature, has desecrated the face of Mother Earth. The white man's advanced technological capacity has occurred as a result of his lack of regard for the spiritual path and for the way of all living things. The white man's desire for material possessions and power has blinded him to the pain he has caused Mother Earth by his quest for what he calls natural resources. And the path of the Great Spirit has become difficult to see by almost all men, even by many Indians who have chosen instead to follow the path of the white man....

Today the sacred lands where the Hopi live are being desecrated by men who seek coal and water from our soil that they may create more power for the white man's cities. This must not be allowed to continue for if it does, Mother Nature will react in such a way that almost all men will suffer the end of life as they now know it. The Great Spirit said not to allow this to happen even as it was prophecied to our ancestors. The Great Spirit said not to take from the Earth —

not to destroy living things. The Great Spirit, Massau'u, said that man was to live in Harmony and maintain a good clean land for all children to come. All Hopi People and other Indian Brothers are standing on this religious principle and the Traditional Spiritual Unity Movement today is endeavoring to reawaken the spiritual nature in Indian people throughout this land. Your government has almost destroyed our basic religion which actually is a way of life for all our people in this land of the Great Spirit. We feel that to survive the coming Purification Day, we must return to the basic religious principles and to meet together on this basis as leaders of our people.

Today almost all the prophecies have come to pass. Great roads like rivers pass across the landscape; man talks to man through the cobwebs of telephone lines; man travels along the roads in the sky in his airplanes; two great wars have been waged by those bearing the swastika or the rising sun; man is tampering with the Moon and the stars. Most men have strayed from the path shown us by the Great Spirit. For Massau'u alone is great enough to portray the way back to Him.

It is said by the Great Spirit that if a gourd of ashes is dropped upon the Earth, that many men will die and that the end of this way of life is near at hand. We interpret this as the dropping of atomic bombs on Hiroshima and Nagasaki. We do not want to see this happen to any place or any nation again, but instead we should turn all this energy for peaceful uses, not for war.

We, the religious leaders and rightful spokesmen for the Hopi Independent Nation, have been instructed by the Great Spirit to express the invitation to the President of the United States and all spiritual leaders everywhere to meet with us and discuss the welfare of mankind so that Peace, Unity, and Brotherhood will become part of all men everywhere.

Sincerely,

(signed) Thomas Banyacya, for
Hopi Traditional Village Leaders:
Mrs. Mina Lansa, Oraibi
Claude Kawangyawma, Shungopavy
Starlie Lomayaktewa, Mushongnovi
Dan Katchongva, Hotevilla

Navajo

Much of their [the Indians'] present economy is based upon reaction and adjustment to racism . . . . Recent events . . . indicate a possible disturbance of this equilibrium. It is difficult to predict how great the disturbance will be or if it will greatly affect the life of the American Indian.

Lionel de Montigny (Métis)

NOTES

Page 16 Frances Densmore, in her monograph *Teton Sioux Music* discusses at length the meaning among the Sioux of Wakan tanka. "In old times," she writes, "the term Wankan'tanka was not used in ordinary conversation, because it was held too sacred to be spoken except with due reverence and at a proper time." In this connection, she continues, "it will be recalled that many tribes of Indians avoid mentioning a man's name, especially in his presence. That which remains unspoken must be considered in the study of any deep phase of Indian thought. A full and complete expression is not in accordance with Indian custom. The unspoken element may be a matter of mutual understanding, no indication of which appears in words, or it may be something which is indicated in such a manner as to be intelligible only to those for whom it is intended. Thus there is a 'sacred language' used by medicine men in which familiar words take on an occult meaning. In attempting to express the meaning of the word *wakan* the following statement was made by several old Indians after consultation: 'An ordinary man has natural ways of doing things. Occasionally there is a man who has a gift for doing extraordinary things, and he is called *wakan*. Although this is a supernatural gift, he can use it only by effort and study. A man may be able to do things in a mysterious way, but none has ever been found who could command the sun and moon or change the seasons. The most wonderful things which man can do are different from the works of nature. When the seasons changed we regarded it as a gift from the sun, which is the strongest of all mysterious *wakan* powers.' In another conversation of the subject it was said: 'We use the words Taku wakan for anything which we can see for ourselves has mysterious power. Thus a pipe is Taku wakan, for with it supplications may be made and good obtained. We can not see the thunder, and we say it is *wakan,* but we see the lightning and we know that the thunder and the lightning are a sign of rain, which does good to the earth. Anything which has similar power is *wakan,* but above all is the sun, which has most power of all.' Other conversations, similar to the preceding, expressed the conviction in the minds of the Sioux that their people had always believed in a mysterious power whose greatest manifestation is the sun, and that Wakan'tanka was the designation of that power."

Densmore also describes the Sioux belief in sacred stones.

"Large stones or rocks in the field were 'objects of worship' among the Sioux Indians. Writing in 1880, Stephen Riggs observed that 'large bowlders were selected and adorned with red and green paint, whither the Dakota might go to pray and offer his sacrifice.' An interesting account of such a stone, known as Eyay Shah, 'Red Rock,' is given by H.C. Hovey in 1887. This stone was situated near the site of St. Paul, Minnesota, and was last visited by the Sioux shortly before their outbreak in 1862. Many stones of the Dakota Prairie are said to have been similarly regarded by the Sioux. To talk of these stones is 'sacred talk' to the Sioux.

"To dream of the sacred stones was considered a great honor. Dreams were sought by the Sioux, but it was recognized that the dream would correspond to the character of the man. Thus it was said that 'a young man would not be great in mind so his dream would not be like that of a chief; it would be ordinary in kind, yet he would have to do whatever the dream directed him to do.' The first obligation of a dream was usually its announcement to the tribe. This was by means of a performance which indicated the nature of the dream and allied the man to others who had similar dreams. If the dream were connected with the sacred stones, or with herbs or animals concerned in the treatment of the sick, it was considered obligatory that the man avail himself of the supernatural aid vouchsafed to him in the dream, and arrange his life in accordance with it. The obligation of a dream was as binding as the necessity of fulfilling a vow, and disregard of either was said to be punished by the forces of nature, usually by a stroke of lightning." (Frances Densmore, *Teton Sioux Music,* Bulletin 61, Bureau of American Ethnology, Washington D.C., pp 157, 206.)

Page 25 Natalie Curtis in *The Indian's Book* writes: "Not all songs are religious, but there is scarcely a task, light or grave, scarcely an event, great or small, but has its fitting song. In nearly every Indian myth the creator *SINGS* things into life. To the Indian, truth, tradition, history, and thought are preserved in ritual of poetry and song. The red man's song records the teachings of his wise men, the great deeds of his heroes, the counsel of his seers, the worship of his God." (*The Indian's Book,* New Edition: Dover, New York, 1968, p. xxiv.)

"I have always been a poor man. I do not know a single song," said a Navaho informant to W.W. Hill, as he began his account of agricultural practices. "It is impossible," continues Dr. Hill, "to state too strongly the belief as illustrated by that statement. It summed up in a few words the whole attitude of the Navaho toward life and the possibility of success. With respect to agriculture, it was not the vicissitudes of environment that made for successful crops or failures, but the control of the natural forces through ritual." (*The Agricultural and Hunting Methods of the Navaho Indians,* Yale University Press, New Haven, 1938, p. 52. Cited in Margot Astrov [ed.] American Indian Prose and Poetry, p. 21.)

Knud Rasmussen records a great hunter's expression of song. "My breath — this is what I call this song," said Orpingalik in 1923, a shaman and poet of the Netsilingmiut Eskimo, "for it is just as necessary to me to sing it as it is to breathe," and then began: "I will sing this song, a song that is strong. . . ."

"Songs," added Orpingalik, "are thoughts, sung out with the breath when people are moved by great forces and ordinary speech no longer suffices. Man is moved just like the ice floe sailing here and there out in the current. His thoughts are driven by a flowing force when he feels joy, when he feels sorrow. Thoughts can wash over him like a flood, making his blood come in gasps, and his heart throb. Something, like an abatement in the weather, will keep him thawed up. and then it will happen that we, who always think we are small, will feel still smaller. And we will fear to use words. But it will happen that the words we need will come of themselves. When the words we want to use shoot up of themselves — we get a new song." ("The Netsilik Eskimos, Social Life and Spiritual Culture," *Report of the Fifth Thule Expedition 1921-1924,* vol. 8, nos. 1-2, Copenhagen, p. 321.)

Page 37 The following excerpts elucidate the Indian's concept of worship in the form of nature.

"Alice C. Fletcher comments (*Report,* Peabody Museum, vol. III, p. 276) that to the Indian mind, the life of the universe has not been analyzed, classified, and a great synthesis formed of the parts. To him the varied forms are equally important and noble. A devout old Indian said [to her] : 'The tree is like a human being, for it has life and grows; so we pray to it and put our offerings on it that the god may help us.' In the same spirit the apology is offered over a slaughtered animal, for the life of the one is taken to supplement the life of the other, 'that it may cause us to live,' one formula expresses it. These manifestations of life, stopping places of the god, can not therefore be accurately called objects of worship or symbols; they appear to be more like media of communication with the permeating occult force which is vaguely and fearfully apprehended. As a consequence, the Indian stands abreast of nature. He does not face it, and hence can not master or coerce it, or view it scientifically and apart from his own mental and emotional life. He appeals to it, but does not worship it." (James O. Dorsey, *A Study of Siouan Cults,* 11th Annual Report of the Bureau of Ethnology, 1889-1890, Washington, 1894, p. 435.)

In contrast, Claude Levi-Strauss views the passage of the Dakota wiseman as exemplary of "a metaphysical philosophy common to all the Sioux from the Osage in the south to the Dakota in the north, according to which things and beings are nothing but materialized forms of creative continuity." (Claude Levi-Strauss, *Totemism*, Boston, Beacon Press, 1963; p. 98.)

Page 40 The number four is a sacred number for the vast majority of tribes in North America. Paul Radin, the anthropologist, relates an interesting speculation of an old philosophical Oglala Sioux, called Tyon, on the significance of the number:

"In former times the Lakota grouped all their activities by fours. This was because they recognized four directions: the west, the north, the east, and the south; four divisions of time: the day, the night, the moon, and the year; four parts in everything that grows from the ground: the roots, the stem, the leaves, and the fruit; four kinds of things that breathe: those that crawl, those that fly, those that walk on four legs, and those that walk on two legs; four things above the world: the sun, the moon, the sky, and the stars; four kinds of gods: the great, the associates of the great, the gods below them and the spiritkind; four periods of human life: babyhood, childhood, adulthood, and old age; and finally, mankind has four fingers on each hand, four toes on each foot and the thumbs and the great toes taken together form four. Since the great spirit caused everything to be in fours, mankind should do everything possible in fours." (Paul Radin, *Primitive Man as Philosopher,* New York and London, D. Appleton, 1927, p. 278.)

Page 42 "One of the symbols that expresses most completely the Plains Indian concept of the relationship between man and the world of nature surrounding him is a cross inscribed within a circle. The symbol is painted on a number of ritual objects, and on the bodies and heads of men who participate in tribal ceremonies. Its form is reflected in the circular shape and central fire of the teepee, the Indian's home; its pattern is found in the Sun Dance and purification lodges and in many of the ritual movements. For example, in the Hako ceremony of the Pawnee, the priest draws a circle on the earth with his toe; the explanation given was that 'the circle represents a nest, and is drawn by the toe, because the Eagle (symbol of the Great Spirit) builds its nest with its claws. Although we are imitating the bird making its nest, there is another meaning to the action; we are thinking of *TIRAWA* making the world for the people to live in!'

"At the center of the circle, uniting within a point the cross of four directions of space and all the other quaternaries of the Universe, is man. Without the awareness that he bears within himself this sacred center a man is in fact less than man. It is to recall the virtual reality of this center that the Indians have so many rites based on the cross within the circle.

"One of the most precise ritual expressions of this 'centrality' is found in one of the rites of the Arapaho Sun Dance, in which their Sacred Wheel is placed against each of the four sides of a man's body, starting from the feet and moving to the head, and is then turned four times sunwise, until finally it is lowered over the head, with the four attached eagle feathers hanging down over the man's breast, so that he is ritually at the center, a vertical axis to the horizontal." (Joseph Epes

Brown, *The Spiritual Legacy of the American Indian,* Wallingford, Pennsylvania, Pendle Hill Publications, 1964, pp. 13-15. For further reference to the "Hako ceremony of the Pawnee" see Alice C. Fletcher, *The Hako: A Pawnee Ceremony,* 22nd Annual Report of the Bureau of American Ethnology, part 2, 1904.)

Clifford Geertz comments, that for most Oglala, "the circle, whether found in nature, painted on a buffalo skin or enacted in a sun dance, is but an unexamined luminous symbol whose meaning is intuitively sensed, not consciously interpreted. . . . Again and again the idea of a sacred circle, a natural form with a moral import, yields, when applied to the world within which the Oglala lives, new meanings; continually it connects together elements within their experience which would otherwise seem wholly disparate and . . . incomprehensible.

"The common roundness of a human body and a plant stem, of a moon and a shield, of a teepee and a camp-circle give them a vaguely conceived but intensely felt significance. And this meaningful common element, once abstracted, can then be employed for ritual purposes as when in a peace ceremony, the pipe, the symbol of social solidarity, moves deliberately in a perfect circle from one smoker to the next, the purity of the form evoking the beneficence of the spirits — or to construe mythologically the peculiar paradoxes and anomalies of moral experience, as when one sees in a round stone the shaping of power of good over evil." (Clifford Geertz, "Ethos, World-View and the Analysis of Sacred Symbols," in *Man Makes Sense,* Boston, Little, Brown, 1970, pp. 326-327.)

Any tribe when on the annual hunt "camped in a circle and preserved its political division, and the circle was often a ¼ mile or more in diameter. Sometimes the camp was in concentric circles, each circle representing a political group of kindred. The Dakota call themselves the 'seven council fires,' and say that they formerly camped in two divisions or groups, one composed of four and the other of three concentric circles. The Omaha and close cognates, when on the annual buffalo hunt and during the great tribal ceremonies, camped in a circle. Each of the 10 Omaha gentes had its unchangeable place in the line. The women of each gens knew where their tents belonged, and when a camping ground was reached each drove her ponies to the proper place, so that when the tents of the tribe were all up each gens was in the position to which it was entitled by the regulations that were connected with ancient beliefs and customs. For particular ceremonies, especially the great annual sun dance, the Kiowa, Cheyenne and others camped in a circle made up of the different political divisions in fixed and regular order.

"The tribal circle, each segment composed of a clan, gens, or band, made a living picture of tribal organization and responsibilities. It impressed upon the beholder the relative position of kinship groups and their interdependence, both for the maintenance of order and government within and for defense against enemies from without; while the opening to the *EAST* and the position of the ceremonial tents recalled the religious rites and obligations by which the many parts were held together in a compact whole." (Frederick Webb Hodge[ed.], *The Handbook of Indians of Canada.)*

Page 56 For further reference on the dreamer religion see Herbert J. Spinden, *The Nez Perce Indians,* The American Anthropological Association, *Memoirs,* vol. 2, pt. 3, Lancaster, 1908.

178

SOURCES FOR TEXTS

The Morning Sun, the New Sweet Earth and the Great Silence

Page 3 The words of Black Hawk, from the *Autobiography of Black Hawk as dictated by himself to Antoine LeClair,* 1833, Historical Society of Iowa (ed. J.B. Patterson). New Edition: American Publishing Company, Rock Island, Illinois, 1912 (with an introduction by James D. Rishell), pp. 62-63.

5 Winnebago wise saying cited in Melvin Randolph Gilmore, *Prairie Smoke,* Bismarck, North Dakota, 1921, p. 9.

5 Quote from Indian chief to the governor of Pennsylvania. (Cited in Paul Jacobs and Saul Landau with Eve Pell, *To Serve the Devil,* vol. 1, "Natives and Slaves," Vintage Books, New York, 1971, p. xxvii.)

6 Chief Luther Standing Bear, *Land of the Spotted Eagle,* Houghton Mifflin, Boston and New York, 1933, pp. 192-197.

7 Charles Alexander Eastman (Ohiyesa), *The Soul of the Indian,* Houghton Mifflin, Boston, 1911, p. 163.

8 Lawrence Kip, *The Indian Council in the Valley of the Walla Walla,* 1855, p. 22.

10 Proceedings of the New Jersey Historical Society, New Series, vol. 13, 1928, pp. 477-479.

12 Ethel Brant Monture, *Canadian Portraits, Brant, Crowfoot, Oronhyatekha, Famous Indians,* © 1960 by Clarke, Irwin, & Company, Ltd., Toronto, p. 120. Used by permission.

15 The words of the old Wintu woman from Dorothy Lee, *Freedom and Culture,* Prentice-Hall, Englewood Cliffs, New Jersey, 1959, pp. 163-164. Reprinted by permission of the author.

16 Frances Densmore, *Teton Sioux Music,* Bulletin 61, Bureau of American Ethnology, Washington, D.C., 1918, pp. 207-208.

18 Ibid., pp. 172-173.

21 N. Scott Momaday, *The Way to Rainy Mountain,* Copyright 1969, The University of New Mexico Press, p. 5.

22 Natalie Curtis, *The Indian's Book,* Harper & Brother, New York and London, 1907. New Edition: Dover Publications, 1968, New York, p. 11.

23 Grant MacEwan, *Tatanga Mani, Walking Buffalo of the Stonies,* M. J. Hurtig, Ltd., Edmonton, Alberta, 1969, pp. 5, 181. Used with permission.

25 Knud Rasmussen, "Intellectual Culture of the Iglulik Eskimos," *Report of the Fifth Thule Expedition, 1921-1924,* vol. 7, nos. 1-3, Copenhagen, 1930, pp. 122-123.

27 Words of Chief Seattle from *The Washington Historical Quarterly 22,* no. 4 (October 1931), the Washington University State Historical Society, Seattle, Washington.

28 Zephyrin Engelhardt, *San Luis Rey Mission,* James H. Barry, San Francisco, 1921, p. 192. (Cited in Louis Thomas Jones, *Aboriginal American Oratory: the Traditional Eloquence Among the Indians of the United States,* Southwest Museum, Los Angeles, 1965.)

29 Helen Addison Howard, *War Chief Joseph,* The Caxton Printers, 1941, p. 85.

30 Chief Seattle.

31 Jonathan Carver, *Travels Through the Interior Parts of North America in the years 1766, 1767, and 1768,* Dublin, 1779, pp. 374-375. (Cited in Benjamin H. Bissell, *The American Indian in English Literature of the 18th Century,* Yale University Press, New Haven, 1925.) For a discussion as to authorship see E.G. Bourne, "The Travels of Jonathan Carver," in the *American Historical Review,* January 1906, p. 287.

33 William W. Warren, *History of the Ojibways, based upon Traditions and Oral Statements,* 1885; New Edition: Ross & Haines, 1957, *History of the Ojibway Nation,* pp. 72-73.

35 Words of Mato-Kuwapi from Densmore, *Teton Sioux Music,* pp. 95-96.

36   Eastman (Ohiyesa), *The Soul of the Indian,* p. 45.

37   James Owen Dorsey, *A Study of Siouan Cults,* 11th Annual Report of the Bureau of Ethnology, 1889-1890, Washington, D.C., 1894, p. 435. (Cited in Claude Levi-Strauss, *Totemism,* Copyright © 1963 by Beacon Press, p. 98; originally published in France in 1962 by Presses Universitaires de France, under the title *Le Totemisme Aujourd'hui,* Copyright © 1962. Reprinted by permission of Beacon Press.) For further information see Waldemar Bogoras, *Primitive Ideas of Space and Time,* in the *American Anthropologist,* N.S. 27, 1925.

39   Densmore, *Teton Sioux Music,* pp. 95-96.

40   Franz Boas, *Ethnology of the Kwakiutl* (based on data collected by George Hunt), 35th Annual Report of the Bureau of American Ethnology, 1913-1914, Washington D.C., 1921, pp. 617, 618, 619. Material quoted in the introductory note from Erna Gunther, *Further Analysis of the First Salmon Ceremony,* University of Washington Press, Seattle, 1928, p. 142.

42   *Black Elk Speaks, Being the Life Story of a Holy Man of the Oglala Sioux,* as told through John G. Neihardt, Copyright 1961, University of Nebraska Press, Lincoln, 1961, pp. 198-200. Used by permission.

43   Curtis, *The Indian's Book,* p. 49.

The Hairy Man from the East

45   Chief Luther Standing Bear, *Land of the Spotted Eagle.* p. xix.

47   Words of Sitting Bull from Stanley Vestal, *Sitting Bull, Champion of the Sioux,* Houghton Mifflin, Boston and New York, 1932, p. 97.

48   Father Chrestien LeClercq, *New Relation of Gaspesia, with the Customs and Religion of the Gaspesian Indians,* translated and edited by William F. Ganong, The Champlain Society, Toronto, 1910, pp. 104-106.

50   Rueben Gold Thwaites (ed.), *Lahontan's New Voyages to North America,* McClurg, Chicago, 1905, vol. 2, p. 533.

51   George Bird Grinnell, *Pawnee Hero Stories and Folk Tales,* Forest and Stream Publishing Company, New York, 1889. New Edition: University of Nebraska Press, Lincoln, 1961, pp. 258-259.

53   Cited in Dee Brown, *Bury My Heart at Wounded Knee,* Holt, Rinehart and Winston, New York, 1970, p. 316.

54   Helen Addison Howard, *War Chief Joseph,* The Caxton Printers, 1941, p. 84.

56-7   Samuel G. Drake, *Biography and History of the Indians of North America,* Third Edition, O.L. Perkins and Hillard, Gray & Company, Boston, 1834, Book I, Ch. 35, p. 27.

60   Norman B. Wood, *Lives of Famous Indian Chiefs,* American Indian Historical Publishing Company, Aurora, Illinois, 1906, pp. 254-256; and William L. Stone, *Life and Times of Sa-Go-Ye-Wat-Ha, or Red Jacket,* Wiley & Putnam, New York and London, 1841, pp. 189-193.

63   William L. Stone, *Life and Times,* p. 334, See also F.W. Hodge (ed.), *Handbook of American Indians North of Mexico,* Bulletin 30, Bureau of American Ethnology, 1907, vol. 2, pp. 360-363.

64   M.I. McCreight, *Firewater and Forked Tongues, a Sioux Chief Interprets U.S. History,* Trail's End Publishing Company, Pasadena, 1947, p. 61.

66   Samuel Griswold Goodrich, *Lives of Celebrated American Indians,* Bradbury, Soden, Boston, 1843, pp. 179-180.

69   Oral tradition of the Delawares from John Heckewelder, *History, Manners and Customs of the Indian Nations Who Once Inhabited Pennsylvania and the Neighboring States,* Memoirs of the Historical Society of Pennsylvania, 1876, p. 77.

Black Elk Speaks, pp. 8, 9, 62, 217.

Katharine C. Turner, *Red Men Calling on the Great White Father,* Copyright 1951 by the University of Oklahoma Press, p. xiii. Used with permission. See also *Niles's Weekly Register,* 36, no. 36 (June 20 and October 11, 1829).

74 Curtis, *The Indian's Book,* p. 329.

77 W.F. Johnson, *Life of Sitting Bull and History of the Indian War of 1890-91,* Edgewood Publishing Company, 1891, pp. 201-202.

78 *Indian Affairs,* File: Miscellaneous letters, 1812-1869, R.G. 10, vols. 626, 627, 628, The Public Archives of Canada, Ottawa.

81 Thomas Jefferson, *The Writings of Thomas Jefferson,* Taylor and Maury, Washington, D.C., 1854, vol. 8, pp. 308-309.

82 Heckewelder, *Indian Nations,* p. 81.

83 George P. Donehoo, *Carlisle and the Red Men of Other Days,* cited in *The American Indian,* vol. 4, no. 5, February 1930.

85 Drake, *Biography and History,* pp. 100-101.

87 Cited in *The American Indian,* vol. 3, no. 11, August 1929.

88 Charles H.L. Johnston, *Famous Indian Chiefs,* L.C. Page, Boston, 1909, p. 380.

90 Cited in Jacobs and Landau, *To Serve the Devil,* vol. 1, pp. 3-4.

91 John Peter Turner, *The North West Mounted Police 1873-1893,* 2 vols., King's Printer and Controller of Stationery, Ottawa, 1950, vol. 1, p. 368. Reproduced by permission of Information Canada.

92 Public Archives of Canada, among the Confidential Papers of the Department of Justice relative to the Trial of Louis Riel, as quoted in G.F.G. Stanley, *The Birth of Western Canada,* University of Toronto Press, Toronto, 1960.

94 Charles Alexander Eastman (Ohiyesa), *Indian Heroes and Great Chieftains,* Little, Brown, Boston, 1918, p. 102.

96 *Answer to Report of the Honorable Dawes Commission* by Choctaw and Chickasaw Nations of Indians, Pamphlets, no. 7.

99 Chief Luther Standing Bear, *Land of the Spotted Eagle,* p. 250.

100 Lewis H. Morgan, *League of the Ho-De-No-Sau-Nee or Iroquois,* Dodd Mead, New York, 1904, Book 3, pp. 104-105. Also cited in Jacobs and Landau, *To serve the Devil,* vol. 1, pp. 62-63.

102 Frank B. Linderman, *Plenty-Coups, Chief of the Crows,* University of Nebraska Press, 1962, pp. 227-228; see also Charles Hamilton (ed.) *Cry of the Thunderbird,* Macmillan, New York, 1950, under the title of William J. Harsha. For autobiographical details see Norman B. Wiltsey, "Plenty-Coups: Crow Chief," in *Montana,* The Magazine of Western History 13, no. 4 (September 1963), pp. 28-39.

103 Chief Luther Standing Bear, *Land of the Spotted Eagle,* pp. 189-191.

106 MacEwan, *Tatanga Mani,* p. 6.

107 Chief Luther Standing Bear, *Land of the Spotted Eagle,* p. 248.

108 Simmons, ed. *Sun Chief,* p. ix, x (foreword).

110 Eastman (Ohiyesa), *The Soul of the Indian.*

My Voice Is Become Weak

111 Black Hawk, *Autobiography,* p. vii.

113 The words of Chiparopai from Curtis, *The Indian's Book,* p. 569.

114 Morgan, *League of the Ho-De-No-Sau-Nee,* Book 2, pp. 266-267.

115 Cited in *The American Indian,* vol. 2, no. 8, May 1928.

117 Wood, *Famous Indian Chiefs,* p. 261. See Also Stone, *Life and Times,* p. 311.

119 Cited in Brown, *Bury My Heart,* p. 321.

181

120 Howard, *War Chief Joseph,* p. 282. See also U.S. Secretary of War, Report, 1877, p. 630. For further reference on oratory see Herbert J. Spinden, ''The Nez Perce Indians,'' The American Anthropological Association, *Memoirs,* vol. 2, 1908, p. 234. (Cited in Margot Astrov [ed.] *American Indian Prose and Poetry,* Capricorn Books Edition, 1962, p. 87.)

121 Lucullus V. McWhorter, *Hear Me My Chiefs!,* Caldwell, Idaho, 1952, pp. 510, 511.

123 Chief Joseph, ''An Indian's View of Indian Affairs,'' *North American Review* 128, 1879. See also Alvin M. Josephy, Jr., *The Nez Perce Indians and the Opening of the Northwest,* Yale University Press, New Haven and London, 1965.

125 Curtis, *The Indian's Book,* p. 569.

128 *Documents and Official Reports Illustrating the Causes which led to the Revolution in the government of the Seneca Indians, in the year 1848 and to the Recognition of their Representative Republican Constitution, by the Authorities of the United States and of the State of New York,* W.M. Wooddy & Son, Baltimore, 1857, pp. 66-67.

130 A.R. Fulton, *The Red Men of Iowa,* Mills, Des Moines, 1882, p. 238.

131 *Documents and Official Reports,* pp. 56-58.

134 E.A. Brininstool, *Crazy Horse,* Wetzel, Los Angeles, 1949, pp. 53-61. For autobiographical details of Crazy Horse, see pp. 43-48, *Dr. V.T. McGillycuddy's Recollections of the Death of Crazy Horse.*

136 Joseph K. Dixon, *The Vanishing Race,* Doubleday, Page, Garden City, 1913, p. 189.

138 Cited in *The American Indian,* vol. 1, no. 3, December 1926, from ''A Chieftain's 'Farewell Letter' to the American People,'' by Muriel H. Wright.

140 Drake, *Biography and History,* Book 5, Ch. 8, pp. 136-137.

143 Black Hawk, *Autobiography,* p. vii.

144 Turner, *Mounted Police,* vol. 1, p. 584.

145-7 Cited in *The American Indian,* vol. 4, no. 5, February 1930. For further reference see Donald J. Berthrong, *The Southern Cheyennes,* University of Oklahoma Press, Norman, 1963; and Douglas C. Jones, *The Treaty of Medicine Lodge: The Story of the Great Treaty Council as Told by Eyewitnesses,* University of Oklahoma Press, Norman, 1966.

150 *Geronimo: His Own Story* by Geronimo, ed. by S.M. Barrett; newly ed. with an intro. and notes by Frederick W. Turner III; intro. and notes copyright © 1970 by Frederick W. Turner III; E. P. Dutton, New York, pp. 170, 173. Used with permission.

152 *Black Elk Speaks,* pp. 199-200.

154 Barrett, *Geronimo,* p. 69.

155 *Black Elk Speaks,* pp. 278-280.

156 William J. Harsha, *Ploughed Under, The Story of an Indian Chief told by himself,* 1881, pp. 249-250. (Cited in Hamilton [ed.], *Cry of the Thunderbird.)*

157 The words of Tecumseh, *History of the Choctaw, Chickasaw and Natchez Indians,* p. 248.

If We Surrender, We Die

159 Quote of Vine Deloria, Jr., abridged from pp. ix-x in *The New Indians,* by Stan Steiner, Harper & Row, New York. Copyright © 1968 by Stan Steiner. Reprinted by permission.

164 Jacobs and Landau, *To Serve the Devil,* vol. 1, pp. 84-85.

168 Harold Cardinal, *The Unjust Society, The Tragedy of Canada's Indians,* Edmonton, Hurtig, 1969, pp. 27-30.

170 *New York Times,* August 1970.

173 Waubageshig (Harvey McCue), ed., *The Only Good Indian: Essays by Canadian Indians,* copyright 1970, New Press, Toronto, p. 124. Reprinted with permission.

FURTHER READING

The "Old" Indian

This grouping highlights the lives and writings of outstanding Indian figures, some of whose ideas have notably influenced the "New" Indians.

Black Elk. *The Sacred Pipe: Black Elk's Account of the Seven Rites of the Oglala Sioux.* Edited by Joseph Epes Brown. Norman: University of Oklahoma Press, 1953.

—————————— . *Black Elk Speaks: Being the Life of a Holy Man of the Oglala Sioux, as told to John G. Neihardt.* Lincoln: University of Nebraska Press, 1961. This book was originally published in 1932.

Black Hawk (Sauk). *Autobiography of Black Hawk as dictated by himself to Antoine Le Clair.* Edited by J.B. Patterson. Iowa: Historical Society of Iowa, 1833. New Edition: Rock Island, Illinois: American Publishing Company, 1912.

Buffalo Child Long Lance, Chief. (Blackfoot). *Long Lance.* New York: Cosmopolitan Book Corporation, 1928.

—————————— . *Redman Echoes.* Los Angeles: Frank Wiggins Trade School, Dept. of Printing, 1933.

Chief Joseph (Nez Perce). "An Indian's View of Indian Affairs," *North American Review,* vol. 269, April, 1879.

Chona, Maria (Papago). *Autobiography of a Papago Woman.* Edited by Ruth Underhill. Menasha, Wisconsin: The American Anthropological Association, *Memoirs,* vol. 46, 1936.

Copway, George [Kah-Ge-Ga-Gah-Bowh] (Chippewa). *Indian Life and Indian History, by an Indian Author.* Boston: Albert Colby, 1860.

Crashing Thunder (Winnebago). *Crashing Thunder: The Autobiography of a Winnebago,* Edited by Paul Radin. New York: Dover Publications Inc., 1963, a republication of a 1920 edition.

Deloria, Ella Cara (Sioux). *Speaking of Indians.* New York: Friendship Press, 1944.

Eastman, Charles Alexander [Ohiyesa] (Sioux). *From the Deep Woods to Civilization: Chapters in the Autobiography of an Indian.* Boston: Little, Brown, 1916.

—————————— . *Red Hunters and the Animal People.* New York: Harper and Brothers, 1904.

—————————— . *Indian Boyhood.* New York: McClure, 1904.

—————————— . *Soul of the Indian: An Interpretation.* Boston: Houghton Mifflin, 1911.

—————————— . *The Indian Today: The Past and Future of the First American.* Garden City, New York: Doubleday, 1915.

—————————— . *Indian Heroes and Great Chieftains.* Boston: Little, Brown , 1918.

Flying Hawk, Chief. *Firewater and Forked Tongues: a Sioux Indian Interprets United States History.* Edited by M.I. McCreight. Pasadena, California: Trail's End Publishing, 1947.

Geronimo (Apache). *Geronimo's Story of His Life,* as told to and edited by S.M. Barrett. New York: Duffield 1906. New Edition: New York: E.P. Dutton, 1970

A Mohegan-Pequot Diary. Recorded by Frank G. Speck. 43rd Annual Report of the Bureau of American Ethnology, 1925-1926, Report 43.

Parker, Arthur Caswell (Seneca). *The Code of Handsome Lake, The Seneca Prophet.* Albany: New York State Museum, Bulletin 163.

Plenty-Coups (Crow). *Plenty-Coups, Chief of the Crows.* Edited by Frank Bird Linderman. Lincoln: University of Nebraska Press, 1962. Originally published in 1930 as *American, The Life Story of a Great Indian, Plenty-Coups, Chief of the Crows.*

Standing Bear, Luther (Sioux). *My People, the Sioux.* Edited by E.A. Brininstool. Boston and New York: Houghton Mifflin, 1928.

_____ . *Land of the Spotted Eagle.* Boston: Houghton Mifflin, 1933.

Talaysever, Don C., *Sun Chief: The Autobiography of a Hopi Indian.* Edited by Leo W. Simmons. New Haven: Yale University Press, 1942.

Two Paiute Autobiographies, as told to Julian H. Steward. University of California Publications in American Archaeology and Ethnology, vol. 33, no. 5, 1934.

Warren, William W, (Ojibway). *History of the Ojibways, based upon Traditions and Oral Statements,* 1885. New Edition: Ross and Haines, 1957.

The "New" Indian

Cardinal, Harold (Cree). *The Unjust Society, The Tragedy of Canada's Indians.* Edmonton: Hurtig, 1969.

Chief D. Eagle (Sioux). *Winter Count.* Denver: Golden Bell Press, 1968.

Clutesi, George C. (Nootka). *Potlatch.* Sidney, B.C.: Gray's Publishing, 1969.

Deloria, Vine, Jr. (Sioux). *Custer Died for Your Sins: An Indian Manifesto.* New York: Macmillan, 1969.

_____ . *We Talk, You Listen; New Tribes, New Turf.* New York: Macmillan, 1970.

Dunn, Marty. *Red on White, The Biography of Duke Redbird (Mohawk).* Toronto and Chicago: New Press, 1971.

Fredericks, Oswald White Bear (Hopi). *Book of the Hopi,* text by Frank Waters. New York: Viking, 1963.

Long, James Larpenteur (First Boy) (Assinboine). *The Assinboines: From the Accounts of the Old Ones told to First Boy.* Edited and with an introduction by Michael Stephen Kennedy. Norman: University of Oklahoma Press. 1961.

Mitchell, Emerson Blackhorse (Navajo). *Miracle Hill: The Story of a Navajo Boy,* with T.D. Allen. Norman: University of Oklahoma Press, 1967.

Momaday, N. Scott (Kiowa). *House Made of Dawn.* New York: Harper and Row, 1969.

_____ . *The Way to Rainy Mountain.* Albuquerque: University of New Mexico Press, 1969.

Monture, Ethel Brant (Mohawk). *Famous Indians: Brant, Crowfoot, and Oronhyatekha.* Toronto: Clarke, Irwin, 1960.

Mountain Wolf Woman (Winnebago). *Mountain Wolf Woman, Sister of Crashing Thunder: The Autobiography of a Winnebago Woman.* Edited by Nancy Oestreich Lurie. Ann Arbor: University of Michigan Press, 1961.

Ortiz, Alfonso (San Juan Pueblo). *The Tewa World: Space, Being, and Becoming in a Pueblo Society.* Chicago: University of Chicago Press, 1969.

Senungetuk, Joseph (Eskimo). *Give or Take a Century: The Story of an Eskimo Family.* San Francisco: The Indian Historian Press, 1970.

Stands In Timber, John (Cheyenne). *Cheyenne Memories, A Folk History,* with Margot Liberty and Robert M. Utley. New Haven: Yale University Press, 1967.

Steiner, Stan. *The New Indians.* New York: Dell, 1968. This book tells of the survival of the old Indian and the emergence of the new Indian, as told in their own words.

Tatanga Mani (Stoney). *Tatanga Mani, Walking Buffalo of the Stonies.* Edited by Grant MacEwan. Edmonton: Hurtig, 1969.

Yellow Wolf (Nez Perce). *The Last Stand of the Nez Perce: Destruction of a People,* with Harvey Chalmers II. New York: Twayne, 1962.

Anthologies

Astrov, Margot. *American Indian Prose and Poetry: An Anthology.* New York: Capricorn Books, 1962.

Curtis, Natalie. *The Indian's Book: Songs and Legends of the American Indians.* New York: Dover Publications, 1969. This book first appeared in 1907.

Forbes, Jack D. "Voices from Native America," in *The Indian in America's Past.* Englewood Cliffs, N.J.: Prentice-Hall, 1964.

Gooderham, Kent. *I Am an Indian.* London: Dent & Sons, Ltd., 1970.

Hamilton, Charles Everett. *Cry of the Thunderbird: The American Indian's Own Story.* New York: Macmillan, 1950.

Jacobs, Paul and Landau, Saul, with Eve Pell. *To Serve the Devil,* ch. 1, "The Indians," in vol. 1, "Natives and Slaves," New York: Vintage Books, 1971.

Jones, Louis Thomas. *Aboriginal American Oratory.* Los Angeles: Southwest Museum, 1965.

Shoemaker, A.G., *The Red Man Speaks.* Doylestown: Doylestown Printing Shop, Chas. L. Goodman, 1947.

Waubageshig (Harvey McCue), *The Only Good Indian: Essays by Canadian Indians.* Toronto: new press, 1970.